Bet the Farm

HOW FOOD STOPPED BEING FOOD

FREDERICK KAUFMAN

WILEY

John Wiley & Sons, Inc.

Published by John Wiley & Sons, Inc., Hoboken, New Jersey
Published simultaneously in Canada

For general information about our other products and services, please contact our
Customer Care Department within the United States at (800) 762-2974, outside the
United States at (317) 572-3993 or fax (317) 572-4002.

Wiley also publishes its books in a variety of electronic formats and by print-on-demand.
Some content that appears in standard print versions of this book may not be available
in other formats. For more information about Wiley products, visit us at www.wiley.com.

Library of Congress Cataloging-in-Publication Data:
Kaufman, Frederick, date.
    Bet the farm : how food stopped being food / Frederick Kaufman.
      p. cm.
    Includes bibliographical references and index.
    ISBN 978-0-470-63192-8 (cloth); ISBN 978-1-118-25904-7 (ebk);
    ISBN 978-1-118-22080-1 (ebk); ISBN 978-1-118-23459-4 (ebk)
     1. Food industry and trade—Social aspects.   2. Food supply—Social aspects.
     3. Agriculture—Economic aspects.   I. Title.
  HD9000.5.K3725   2012
  338.1—dc23

                                          2012013720

*For Luke Mitchell and
for Lizzie*

Contents

Introduction

Closed to the Press

Winter in the Swiss Alps, and the helicopters settle on landing pads patrolled by troops. Out the doors walk presidents, prime ministers, and the CEOs of companies like Google, ExxonMobil, and Bank of America. More than two thousand international leaders and luminaries have come to the World Economic Forum's annual meeting in Davos, Switzerland, where they will weigh the prospects of the planet and everyone on it—and not necessarily tell us their conclusions.

Journalists trail the global chieftains, but Davos is not the easiest spot for them to ply their trade. Most of the lectures and debates are closed to the press, and all are held under the Chatham House Rule of confidentiality: "Participants are free to use the information received, but neither the identity nor the affiliation of the speaker, nor that of any other participant, may be revealed."

In January 2012, Professor Yaneer Bar-Yam, president of the New England Complex Systems Institute in Cambridge, Massachusetts, came here to speak. The topic of his presentation was not typical for the World Economic Forum—not global capital and risk, not the future of democracy and development. But the seminar room was packed. Yaneer Bar-Yam was going to talk about food.

Everyone who lives eats, so the moguls and the magnates scrutinized the models and graphs Bar-Yam projected on the screen. They sat in silence as the professor proved what everyone in the room already knew. Something had gone wrong with food, and the problem went beyond E. coli or high-fat, high-sugar diets. The problem went beyond artificial ingredients, pesticides, and fast-food restaurants.

The trouble with food, explained Bar-Yam, had first become apparent four years earlier, in 2008. That year, farmers produced more grain than ever, enough to feed twice as many people as were on Earth. In the same year, for the first time in history, a billion people went hungry. The paradox bordered on the pathological.

What had gone wrong with food? The Davos participants believed they understood the issues, and in this regard we have a lot in common with them. Modern food consciousness has been rooted in the writings of Wendell Berry, Frances Moore Lappé, Marion Nestle, Raj Patel, Michael Pollan, and Eric Schlosser, to name but a few. The activist agenda has been set: slow versus fast, small versus big, nutritional versus chemical, organic versus conventional, diversity versus monoculture, sustainable versus wasteful, farm-to-fork versus transnational, and local versus food from nowhere.

But along with our consciousness of the food problem have come a number of assumptions. Some of these have to do with how the problem came to be, others have to do with how the problem affects us, and still others have to do with the solution and how to fight back. Most of that fighting back currently takes place at the cash register as we buy food outside the agro-industrial supply chain and try to eat local and organic food, mostly vegetables. As a general rule, we believe that what ails the system must be either corporate greed or people not knowing any better, so we look to the education system to teach children how to eat and to government regulations to alter the behavior of those who sell us food.

But just as we returned to an appreciation of real food, just as we came to value family farms and local produce, it was as though food had slipped out of our grasp. In 2008, the price of the world's most basic foods doubled, then doubled again, and people like Bar-Yam began to suspect that the problem went further than what we had assumed. The problem went to the core of the global system, and the system was broken.

If you eat the most delicious local, grass-fed filet mignon, grilled with a side of seasonable vegetables and organic herbs, all from your neighborhood green market, that meal has come to you because there was money in it. If your daughter eats a school lunch of low-quality factory-farmed chicken nuggets and a suspicious-looking, peel-open cup of heavily sugared applesauce, all for just $1.50, that meal has come to her because there was money in it.

Food and money go way back, but something had transformed the basic transaction of selling a farm good for more than it cost to plant and harvest. Something had changed the way food is bought and sold. The CEOs at Davos were talking about food because it had stopped acting like food. But how could something so basic turn into something it was not?

Food had been financialized, Bar-Yam explained to the packed room in Davos. Food had become an investment, equivalent to oil, gold, silver, or any other commodity, equity, or derivative. The higher the price, the better the investment. The better the investment, the more costly the food. And those who cannot pay the price pay with hunger.

But financialized food can pose problems for the CEOs of Pepsi and Yum Brands, too. The food business needs food to make food. You can't sell burgers, chicken wings, french fries, Cheerios, or Twinkies if you can't purchase the ingredients, and when the price of fundamental ingredients goes up, profits go down. Today, as half of the world heads toward obesity and the other half toward starvation, it's worth asking who, exactly, is making the money.

For the rising price of food affects the bottom line of some of the largest processors and retailers on Earth. And the heads of Coca-Cola, General Mills, Kraft, and Nestlé understood that in order to solve their problem they would need to know why the price had come undone. They would need to quantify every cause and every effect.

And that was what Professor Bar-Yam was doing at Davos. He had translated food into numbers, reduced it to data. And this the Davos crowd could comprehend. But as subtly as he could, Bar-Yam was also pointing fingers. He'd figured out who was at the bottom of this. His tale had a villain—or villains—and some of them were no doubt in attendance.

PART I

Looking for a Slice

Understanding the causation of hunger . . . calls for an analysis of the entire economic mechanism.

— Amartya Sen, *Development as Freedom*, 1999

1

A Marvel
of Technology

had thought it was a simple question: Why can't inexpensive, healthy, and delicious food be available to everyone?
And I thought I had a simple answer: pizza. According to the pizza industry, pizza is the world's most popular food, a thirty-six-billion-dollar-a-year business. If anything could feed everybody, it was pizza.

The Japanese go for slices topped with eel and squid, while Bangkok residents like their crusts folded around hot dogs. Pakistani pizza features curry, Costa Rican pizza features coconut, and Hong Kong locals have discovered a taste for abalone, crayfish, and crab roe pizza. Russians like their pizza topped with sardines and onions. Depending on where you stand on planet Earth, you may find yourself contemplating a slice of bacon cheeseburger pizza; dandelion pizza; mashed potato pizza; pulled-pork pizza; pickled ginger, minced mutton, and tofu pizza; or peanut butter and jelly pizza.

According to a recent Gallup Poll, children ages three to eleven prefer pizza over all other foods for lunch and dinner. So if you happen to be contemplating pizza, you may be standing in a school lunch line. And since a school lunch must include a serving of vegetables, it was only a matter of time before the following question arose: Is pizza a vegetable? The U.S. Congress and the U.S. Department of Agriculture spent a great deal of time and energy last year considering this question.

For the record, pizza is not a vegetable. But there was something lost amid the uproar over just how many tomatoes might or might not have given their lives to the pizza sauce atop a schoolkid's lunchtime slice. Lost amid the fight over high sodium, childhood obesity, and pizza industry lobbyists was the question of eleven billion dollars of federal school lunch money—a great portion of it embedded in frozen pizza.

We are talking about a lot of cash. The global pizza market is roughly equivalent to the gross domestic product of Lithuania. Pizza is big, but in order to satisfy the appetite of everyone on Earth, pizza would have to be even bigger. Fortunately, the bigger the pizza business, the more profitable the pizza business—which meant there might be money in feeding the world.

Recently, Domino's Pizza CEO J. Patrick Doyle returned from New Delhi, India, where he had opened his company's nine thousandth franchise and unveiled the next phase in his master strategy for global pizza domination. The company would establish a foothold of restaurants in Malaysia while doubling the number of U.K. locations by 2017. "We're in sixty-five countries right now," announced Doyle. "We're not seeing many places where it doesn't make sense for Domino's Pizza to go." Of course, where's there's lots of money, lots of people want in.

The international taste for slices fuels a global melee for market share among four players: Domino's, Pizza Hut, Papa John's, and Little Caesars. These companies compete for billion-dollar pizza delivery markets everywhere—markets known inside the industry as "couch commerce." And so the day after Doyle opened the nine thousandth Domino's, archrival Pizza Hut countered with an announcement of its own plans to open four hundred new delivery outlets throughout India by the end of the next fiscal year.

This meant war. But it also meant more pizza for more people. And perhaps it might mean less expensive pizza for more people. A pizza war might even mean healthier, more delicious meals for everyone on Earth—which was what I was looking for, the answer to the food question. So I visited the front line.

I inched my rental car through an industrial park outside Detroit and pulled up in front of a low-slung monster of a shed that housed one of Domino's seventeen U.S. pizza dough distribution facilities. These centers dot the United States and furnish all the goods for twice-a-week deliveries to five thousand Domino's retail pizza outlets across the nation. Half of the company's U.S. employees are truck drivers, and Domino's eighteen-wheelers cover eighteen to twenty million miles a year delivering ingredients. These trucks average a little under six miles per gallon. Way back in 1960, Domino's founders, brothers Tom and James Monaghan, purchased their first pizza joint not all that far from this forsaken stretch of Michigan frost and weed. Today the chain employs more than ten thousand people, and its 2010 fiscal revenue topped $236 million.

I was met by Domino's public relations manager, Chris Brandon, an enthusiastic twentysomething who led the way into an antiseptic dough-making room of clattering conveyor belts, industrial mixers, precision cutters, and metal detectors. Domino's manufactures its product in a place that looks nothing like a wheat field, a tomato farm, a dairy, or a kitchen. Every half second or so, a warm ball of Domino's pizza dough emerged at the end of the assembly line. Later, I did a few calculations and figured that if each of Domino's seventeen U.S. distribution centers were creating pizza dough at this rate for eight-hour shifts, five days a week, the company had to be selling around a million pizza pies each day in this country.

Ever good-natured, Brandon grabbed one of the just-manufactured dough balls and threw it to me like a baseball. Then he explained that each lump must be X-rayed before it can be released into the world, just in case a tooth-crushing twist of metal or a stomach-puncturing screw might have fallen off the assembly line and dropped into the mix.

I was impressed, and I became even more impressed when I approached a tremendous stainless-steel tureen that stood as high as my chest. A carefully calibrated stream of water flushed into the bowl, and after the water came an autodispensed dose of soy crush—commonly known as vegetable oil—that turned the liquid a dull yellow. Then five hundred pounds of industrial flour exploded out of yet another stainless-steel pipe. Through billowing clouds of white I glimpsed the computer that ran the proprietary Domino's software. "Step #17," read the screen. "Adding Flour."

Then it was time for a lifting machine to hoist the quarter-ton glob of dough fifteen feet into the air and for a tilting machine to tip the entire concoction out of the tureen and into an enormously large stainless-steel hopper. "It's going to miss the bowl," I said.

"It may look that way," Brandon reassured me, "but it never misses." The dough slithered out of the tureen and into the center of the hopper. He smiled.

But a few minutes later, the next five-hundred-pound batch hit the metal ledge of the hopper, slid off the side, and unceremoniously plopped onto the factory floor. Red lights flashed, alarm bells rang, the production line jolted to a halt, and Brandon stared as a great white blob slowly distended across the cement. For the first time in recorded history, a batch of Domino's pizza dough had missed the bowl.

Brandon ushered me away from the slowly spreading ooze and through a few sets of blue canvas automatic roll-up doors to a warehouse infused with the aroma of garlic, peppers, and onions. We were joined by Larry Manning, yet another customer relations expert, who explained that along with yeast, water, wheat, flour, and soy crush, pizza dough requires salt, sugar, and the "goody bag"—the top-secret potpourri that makes a Domino's dough rise above the rest. These are the elements that must be on hand at all times in order to create Domino's pizza—not to mention a million or so cardboard boxes. Big Pizza means packaged pizza, and that means money spent on cardboard. "You've got some major players out there," said Manning.

I noticed a small black disk attached to one side of his tennis shoes. "It's called a step tracker," Manning said, and he explained that true to its name, the step tracker tracked every step he took. "This is to get people energized, motivated, moving."

Not every Domino's employee has a disk attached to the shoe. But for those who do, Domino's has connected step-tracker readers to the USB ports of selected computers. Whenever Manning or another step-tracked employee walks by one of these computers, the reader downloads the latest step-track data to a Domino's Pizza website, where it is easy to track who has taken the most or the least number of paces for Domino's that day, that hour, that week, or that year.

In the ten-thousand-year history of agriculture, had any peasant, grain merchant, or chef ever counted his or her steps? Not until today, when the footsteps of Domino's employees join Domino's ever expanding database of truck fuel, garlic powder, blocks of mozzarella, wheat prices, and every other conceivable component of a pizza that could be stuffed into a computer.

Manning told me that Domino's management had divided Domino's employees into step-tracking teams—who were at that very moment competing for a variety of step-tracking prizes, such as discounted health insurance. In order to win a prize, every team member would have to take a minimum of 323,000 steps. "It makes you walk," said Manning.

With renewed purpose, we strode past pallet after pallet of dressings, spices, and countless cases of a product named Pizza Sauce Ready to Use, a tomato topping produced by a company called Paradise Tomato Kitchens, based in Louisville, Kentucky. I began to consider how much of everything it would take to keep the entire world in pizza. How many steps? How many cans of tomato sauce? How many tomatoes in each can? And where did all those tomatoes come from? And how were they grown?

I was obsessing over the tomatoes, hardly aware that Manning had changed the subject. "And we got *blown out* of our hedges," he said. I had no idea what he was talking about, but the obnoxious little black disk on his shoe made everything Manning said seem absurd, so I did not ask him about hedges and why Domino's Pizza had gotten blown out of them.

I still thought that feeding the world was about the food. I still thought that pizza was about the dough, the garlic powder, and the blocks of mozzarella, and maybe something more about cardboard boxes and trucks.

A few weeks later I called the Paradise tomato sauce people in Louisville and learned that Pizza Sauce Ready to Use was a marvel of technology. "A great pizza sauce is custom designed to work optimally with the dough, the cheese, and the pizza oven," said Justin Uhl, the head of research and development at Paradise Tomato Kitchens. Uhl's careful choice of words—the language of industrially designed tomato sauce precisely fitted to Domino's industrial standards—was my first clue that the transnational pizza producer's tomato did not have much in common with the tomato of the roadside farm stand. But I was heartened to hear about vegetables rather than eighteen wheelers, cardboard boxes, and step tracking. At least this was an indication of the path of pizza back to the farm. There is an old journalistic adage: "Follow the money." My rule now became "Follow the tomatoes."

But following the tomatoes was not simple. I was surprised to discover that numerous books and treatises have been written on the subject. Websites and dissertations have been devoted to the planting, reaping, buying, and selling of tomatoes. Most recently, Barry Estabrook traced the struggles of underpaid tomato pickers in Florida and gave his book the apt title *Tomatoland: How Modern Industrial Agriculture Destroyed Our Most Alluring Fruit* (2011). For the commercial tomato business is like a country unto itself. It is colossal—and has been for a long time.

For the past hundred years or so, the ever improving proficiencies of fertilizing, irrigating, slicing, dicing, and pureeing have enabled the tomato to become the vegetable kingdom's greatest international commodity, with the bulk of the sauce and salsa spurting from the stainless-steel condensers of factories owned by some of the biggest names in global food, industrial titans such as Del Monte, Heinz, and Unilever.

But of the four thousand kinds of tomatoes on the planet, only a select few hybridized, high-yield, high-pulp varieties—the AB2, the Sun 6366, and the Asgrow 410—will make it into the global market for tomato sauce. These varieties are the so-called process tomatoes, and only they will be transformed into the earth's supply of ketchup, tomato paste, tomato soup, and pizza topping. And with all of the scientific research and product development devoted to engineering the tomato seeds of the future, with all of the far-flung transportation networks and hundreds of millions of transnational dollars committed to the tomato-industrial complex, it is easy to forget the humble origins of the fruit.

The earliest known specimens of *Solanum lycopersicum* flourished in the thin air of Bolivia, Ecuador, and Peru before they migrated to Mexico, where the Mayans became enchanted with the marble-sized fruit and devoutly copied its likeness onto their ancient cookware. The Spanish conquistador Hernán Cortés was the first European to buy the product; he purchased *xtomatl* seeds in the great market of Chichén

Itzá and brought them back with him across the Atlantic, where Old World botanists analyzed the New World rarities shaped like human hearts, and declared them aphrodisiacs.

Throughout the majority of the tomato's postcolonial career in North America, the general public considered the "wolf peach," lethal, perhaps because of its poisonous cousins in the nightshade family, belladonna and mandrake. But after a while, almost everyone realized that even though the deadly aphrodisiac was neither deadly nor aphrodisiacal, there was money in it. By the early twentieth century the H. J. Heinz Company was producing twelve million bottles of ketchup each year and exporting it to Australia, India, Japan, South Africa, and any other international market it could find. Today, as salsa overtakes ketchup in the race for global supremacy, the process tomato reigns as an undisputed supermarket superstar, a staple of Mediterranean and Latin American diets and the essential ingredient of pizza topping. The earth's annual production of the Peruvian fruit now exceeds a hundred million tons, and the demand continues to grow.

Certain parts of the world profit from and delight in the economic efficiencies of the commercialized, homogenized, globalized tomato. "The founding of Paradise Tomato Kitchens was rooted in innovation and technology," the company's CEO, Ron Peters, explained in an e-mail. "With the economic challenges our customer base faces, it is our mission to help be the driving engine in our shared success."

The customer base and the economic challenges that matter to Peters and Paradise Tomato Kitchens are the corporate concerns of Domino's Pizza, Pizza Hut, Papa John's, and Little Caesars—not the people who actually grow tomatoes or buy them at the supermarket. Then again, no one would expect Paradise to care too much about keeping the rest of the world's tomato purveyors and processors in business. The people at Paradise have plenty to keep themselves occupied as they enhance their sauce technologies and expand their market share. And lucky for Paradise, every year Domino's, Pizza Hut, and the rest of the international brotherhood of Big Pizza require ever increasing tonnages of custom-designed industrial tomato sauce.

One very big step down from those who purchase, process, and distribute global tomato sauce are those across the globe who sow, reap, and sell plain old tomatoes. And somewhere between the local market and the global market emerges a food paradox. This paradox is economic, and it borders on the ludicrous: the ever increasing international demand for designer tomatoes, custom grown for processors, has made it all but impossible for small- and medium-size tomato farms to sell what they grow.

If a chef decides she will only cook what she can get at the farmers' market, her pizza may taste different from month to month or week to week. There's absolutely nothing wrong with that. But industrial food depends on uniform ingredients, consistent components that have become the food industry's "widget," a word that entered the language in a 1924 Broadway comedy (*Beggar on Horeseback* by George Kaufman and Marc Connelly) and now means just about anything that comes from a factory—or in this case, a factory farm. Domino's, Pizza Hut, and Papa John's need last week's tomato paste to look, taste, and pour just like this week's tomato paste.

If you buy a slice in Tulsa or Tokyo, you expect it to taste the same as the slice you buy in Brooklyn or Bangkok. In fact, consistency of product is one of the reasons you choose to spend your lunch money at Domino's, Pizza Hut, or Papa John's.

Of course, it's hard enough to make the pizza taste exactly the same every day at just one pizzeria in Jersey City, let alone across the continents. Industrial food companies replicate taste on a global scale, and it is a marvel of technology. But food widgets lead to the paradox.

Uniform size, consistent skin, and compatible pulp mean getting rid of farmers who plant their own seeds, use their own methods, or experiment with anything that's going to keep them from harvesting tons of transportable, reliable, congruous widgets. Consistency spells the end for small farmers who produce the kind of tomatoes their grandparents produced. And since the tomato story has gone global, the demand for designer sauce components doesn't just mean that a few farmers in California will have to find new jobs. The global tomato has global effects: big tomato kills small tomato.

In Ghana, for example, locally harvested tomatoes were once an inexpensive, healthy, and delicious dietary staple. But tens of thousands of tons of imported tomato concentrate made from pulpy, hybrid, high-tech, low-juice, pizza-ready, taxpayer-subsidized process tomatoes have destroyed the market for locally grown tomatoes, not to mention the lives of the nearly two million people involved in tomato cultivation in Ghana's northern provinces. Despite its tomato-farming tradition, Ghana has become the world's second largest *importer* of process tomatoes, after Germany. As a result, countless tomato farmers have gone belly-up.

Comfort Mantey, a tomato farmer in the Ghanaian community of Matsekope, was one of a few dozen people interviewed by field-workers from the global poverty agencies who flock to the tomato fields as the annual farming disaster unfolds. "We do not get good prices for the little harvest," said Mantey.

"The traders tell us their customers now mix fresh tomatoes with imported tomato paste."

Another tomato farmer, Martin Pwayidi, defaulted on the two-thousand-dollar loan he had secured from a bank and sunk into his four acres. No one would buy locally grown tomatoes from him. "I lost everything," Pwayidi told a reporter from one of the few African news outlets covering the story. "There was absolutely no reason to live."

A similar conclusion has been reached by many of Pwayidi's neighbors, and annual waves of suicides wash across Ghana's northern growing regions. Desperate farmers have chosen a symbolic way of killing themselves: as Socrates drank hemlock, tomato farmers drink the insecticide no longer needed for their crops. Others flee their land for the city, where frozen pizza awaits in supermarkets and take-out pizza comes boxed and hot. But more often than not, those who once sold tomatoes in the country cannot make enough money to buy tomato sauce in the city.

The more tomato sauce, the fewer tomato farmers. But perhaps this is a small price to pay, considering that Big Pizza delivers to the world an unprecedented abundance of cheap, delicious food.

2

The Domino's Effect

Take-out pizza isn't really the solution to world hunger, no matter how good a solution it may be to Friday night suburban hunger. Pizza won't solve the larger problem, but everyone at the top of the corporate food ladder believes that the dynamics of couch commerce clue us in to the global solution: buy it cheaper, make it cheaper, ship it cheaper, sell it cheaper. It's hard to argue the point when so many people enjoy so much food made so quickly for so little. And the companies are making a lot of food.

About half of the U.S. milk supply is used to manufacture cheese, and 2009's ten billion pounds broke all previous production records. Mozzarella recently topped cheddar as the most popular cheese variety. And where does all that mozza-rella go? Onto mass-produced pizza, of course.

The time had come for me to "follow the cheese." Every shred of Domino's cheese comes from a Denver-based com-pany called Leprino Foods, the world's largest producer of mozzarella, with sales estimated at $2.6 billion in 2009. At one point, the company held more patents related to mozza-rella cheese than anyone else in the industry—not to mention its patents for lactose derivatives and whey proteins (for use in baby formula and animal feed). Leprino also happens to be one of the largest privately held companies in the United States, and its employees are notorious for not speaking to the press. "We'd prefer to stay under the radar," a Leprino vice president told the *Denver Business Journal* in 2002.

My own repeated attempts to contact James Leprino, the mozzarella billionaire the *Denver Post* once dubbed "Den-ver's Biggest Cheese," took me up a ladder of increasingly paranoid cheese executives until I found someone who was quite willing to talk to me for an hour—off the record. I learned that in order to supply mozzarella to Domino's, Pizza Hut, and almost everyone else in the global pizza industry, one company, Leprino, must buy 5 to 7 percent of the total available milk in the United States. One out of every twenty U.S. milk cow udders must be dedicated to the output of the global pizza machine in the form of James Leprino's patented, easy-freeze, easy-melt mozzarella.

The ancient Romans manufactured cheese. So did the ancient Greeks, the ancient Egyptians, the Sumerians of Mesopotamia, and our ancestors who roamed the prehistoric grasslands of the Sahara. Cheese may be the world's oldest pro-cessed food. But like the new transnational tomato, industrial cheese has moved beyond the realm of food to the realm of global trade, commerce, and commodity. "Commodities are Moveables, valuable by Money," John Locke declared in *Economic Writings and Two Treatises of Government* in 1691—less than a century after the birth of Parmesan and just about two centuries before the first documented use of mozzarella on a pizza, in 1889.

The result of the world's massive demand for cheese is that the product has become both food and finance. Still, it may come as a shock that forty-pound blocks of cheddar are traded on the Chicago Mercantile Exchange along with propane, platinum, and U.S. Treasury bills. The price of commodity milk also appears on the big board. The so-called hundred-weight, or one-hundred-pound measure, of milk is the outcome of complex financial calculations: the product of skim milk prices, butterfat prices, protein prices, whey prices, and the "somatic cell adjustment rate," which is the price of cheese multiplied by 0.0005, then rounded to the fifth decimal place. And that is the simplified version.

Such are the things pizza pros talk about when they talk about pizza. For the manufacture of Domino's, Pizza Hut, and Papa John's has become less about food and more about numbers, indexes, sums, rates, and formulas that are impossible for anyone but an expert to understand. Pizza has become an equation.

But after all of the complexity comes simplicity. It's all about the price, and the day-to-day dollar-and-cent movement of industrial cheese traded on the Chicago Mercantile Exchange has been put into the hands of the world's biggest buyers and processors, companies like Leprino, Dean Foods, and Kraft (the maker of Cool Whip, Kool-Aid, Cheese Whiz, and more than a hundred other brands, twelve of which generate yearly revenues that exceed a billion dollars).

Of course, it is in the best interests of these very large corporations to keep the price of their essential component, milk, as low as possible. And as absurd as it may sound, this priority has led to monopolistic trading practices on the dairy exchanges in Chicago that have forced the price of milk into a downward spiral. In 2008, a group called the Dairy Farmers of America (DFA) paid a twelve-million-dollar penalty for trying to manipulate prices. In 2012, seven thousand farmers brought a class action suit against the DFA, alleging that once again it was manipulating milk prices, this time in cahoots with Dean Foods.

Financialized food is volatile, and even a small dip in the price of bulk milk can mean significant profits for those who buy a few swimming pools' worth, process the lot into cheese, and sell it to the companies that sell the slices. And even though no one in the food business has a monopoly on the product, we're seeing an increase in monopolylike power. The fewer places a farmer has to sell his or her milk, the harder it is to drive a good bargain. Even the manufacturers and processors have fewer places to sell their products as more and more food is sold at slimmer profit margins to a decreasing number of chain restaurants and massive grocery stores.

Milk lies near the bottom of the food chain. Perhaps that is why the fairness of the price does not matter to those near the top. But bottomed-out milk prices are not a good thing for everybody. As milk has been reduced to a flickering line of numbers on a computer screen, the huge conglomerates have forced out scores of small-scale milk processors and milk trucking companies. In all, more than seventy-one thousand small U.S. dairy farms have been pushed from the milk business.

It's the same paradox as with process tomatoes. As the largest of the pizza transnationals demand more and more milk for more and more mozzarella for the world's ever expanding appetite for pizza, the ever descending price of milk has devastated those without whom there would be no milk, no mozzarella, and no pizza. Just as global tomato sauce everywhere has cursed small-scale tomato growers anywhere, Leprino's demand for milk has condemned the small-scale dairy farmer. The more milk, the less milk.

When he is not tending his own cows, John Bunting, a dairyman from the western foothills of the Catskills in New York State, writes a blog about the life of U.S. dairy farmers. "I am old enough to remember when dairy farm communities prospered," he told me. But as the price of milk has touched bottom, New York State's dairy farms have battled bankruptcy. "There is no one in the country making a living milking cows," he said. "Not this year and not last year, either. I get calls every day from just plain desperate farmers. Nobody knows what to do. Farmers have never received less money for their milk."

But as the country's small-scale dairy farmers head into debt, the largest producers of cheese have prospered. "Kraft and Leprino are on tight margins," said Bunting, "but they have so many units running past the cash register that Jimmy Leprino can get rich."

Despite the unprofitability of cow milking, one upstate New York dairy farmer, Dean Pierson, refused to let go of the fifty-one cows on the land his father had bought. Instead, Pierson took a small-caliber rifle off his rack and went through the barn he had built and shot each of his animals through the head. Then he sat down on a chair and put a bullet through his chest. Farmer suicides, no longer confined to the hinterlands of Ghana, had reached the United States.

"The milk-pricing system is truly an attack on the family farm," Bunting said, "and truly an attack on the family that operates the farm." As more and more dairy farmers lose more and more money every day of every month, the self-destructive illogicality of global pizza becomes clear. The day I spoke to Bunting, he told me that five giant dairy operations in the Texas panhandle had just declared bankruptcy. "The system is breaking down," he said. "And no one seems to be paying attention."

On top of the world's most popular pizza, above the mozzarella, above the tomatoes and the lowly wheat, sit sovereign slices of protein known as pepperoni. This crown of protein embodies the world's ever increasing fixation on consuming animal flesh, an obsession that sounds more like a psychological syndrome than a dietary preference. In India and China, the two indicators that mark entrance to the middle class are car ownership and increased meat consumption. As a result, Pizza Hut alone dishes out more than seven hundred million pounds of industrial pepperoni each year, a meat that knows no place of origin or season.

Every day, countless cylinders of proto-pepperoni extrude from protein factories across the land. The tubes ferment and age, then travel to the slicers and dicers that hew innumerable diameters and thicknesses, each ingeniously calibrated to resist cupping, charring, and the dreaded grease-out. Dried, frozen, or "heat and serve," packed by the case and delivered by the truckload, pizza equals pepperoni, pepperoni equals meat, and meat equals middle class.

Meat equals other things, too. More than any other culinary addiction of the most affluent billion people on Earth, meat eating has become the focal point of anger. The food movement has zeroed in on the environmental disaster of raising industrial cattle in concentrated animal feeding operations (aka factory farms), on the public health disaster of meat-borne illnesses, and on the philosophical and ethical question of the living conditions of animals and the pain they feel. Many individuals have expressed their outrage, from the Princeton philosopher Peter Singer to the popular novelist Jonathan Safran Foer to Richard Melville Hall, a musician better known as Moby.

Much less well known is a Canadian academic named Tony Weis, a professor of geography at the University of Western Ontario and an expert on the social, political, demographic, economic, and environmental impacts of meat. "Meat has moved from the periphery of the human diet to its center," he told me on the phone from his office. "But the least efficient converter of feed-to-flesh output is beef cattle."

In other words, it takes an extraordinary amount of diesel fuels, nitrogen fertilizers, pesticides, herbicides, and fungicides and untold gallons of water to create the relatively few calories that the body of a cow can deliver to the body of a human through the pepperoni on a pizza. Less meat production on Earth would not only mean more fresh drinking water for people, but more water to irrigate fields of food destined for human mouths. Less meat production would mean less grain required to feed chickens, hogs, and steers and more corn and wheat for people.

"You have an increasing global demand for pepperoni pizza," said Weis. "How is this going to be sustained with near-term rising energy costs when so much fossil energy is embedded in the pepperoni?" In other words, making food takes energy—from the fuels for tractors and eighteen-wheel delivery trucks to the intensive industrial processes that transform atmospheric nitrogen into synthetic fertilizer. And in the food business, energy has become just another name for money. When the price of crude oil or gasoline rises on the international market, that price becomes an entry on the spreadsheets that define the price of meat. An environmental journalist named Richard Manning summed up the process in the title of his February 2004 article for *Harper's*, "The Oil We Eat."

Animal flesh—like tomatoes, milk, and cheese—has become ever more closely aligned with dollars. When the prices of gold, silver, corn, and wheat skyrocket on the Chicago Mercantile Exchange, so skyrockets the cost of pepperoni—not to mention the price of hamburgers, hot dogs, bacon, pork chops, and chicken wings. After a while, it's hard to perceive that pepperoni was ever part of a beast that roamed the earth. And that may be because pepperoni is not as much an animal as it is a process.

Not many corporations on Earth possess the financial resources and the technical capabilities to deliver tonnages of pepperoni tailored to the demands of Domino's Pizza. So it may come as no surprise that the pepperoni on Domino's comes from the planet's largest purveyor of protein, Tyson Foods. This company has attracted a multitude of detractors and has been blamed for contaminating every lake, river, stream, well, and municipal water supply in Arkansas. Tyson has been accused of animal cruelty and hazardous workplace conditions, sued for releasing carcinogenic arsenic into the atmosphere, and investigated by the U.S. Department of Justice for criminal bribery.

Tyson Foods not only supplies Domino's Pizza with all of its pepperoni, it also supplies Kentucky Fried Chicken with all of its chicken. The company, which employs more than a hundred thousand people, entered the pepperoni business in 2001, when it outbid the Wall Street leveraged-buyout specialists Donaldson, Lufkin & Jenrette and fellow protein producer (and archenemy) Smithfield Foods to acquire a company named Iowa Beef Packers, which up until then had been the nation's leading producer of beef and pork, the essential components of pepperoni.

Tyson put up almost four and a half billion dollars in cash, stock, and debt for the deal, but when the papers were signed Tyson realized it had overpaid for the pepperoni and tried to back out of the agreement. A court in Delaware ruled that Tyson had come down with a classic case of buyer's remorse. The company had to take home what it had bought. Out of court, Tyson has called the acquisition one of its great corporate triumphs.

Today, not only does Tyson supply Domino's with all the pepperoni it requires, but rumor has it that the world leader in protein deals pepperoni to Domino's main competitors, Pizza Hut and Papa John's. Tyson keeps its customer list confidential.

It was pepperoni that brought me to Tyson's world headquarters in Springdale, Arkansas. The lobby had been painted with the phrase "Powered by Tyson" and a question: "Have you had your protein today?" The corridors popped with an art collection that included masterpieces by Andy Warhol, Willem de Kooning, Roy Lichtenstein, and Robert Motherwell—which is what a corporation can afford for its walls when it sells twelve billion dollars' worth of anything each year.

At the end of one particularly long passageway loomed a strange sphinxlike figure: a cow with the head of a rooster, the essence of Tyson's protein-money machine. Beyond the protein monster, the corridor opened into the most recent architectural addition to Tyson's world headquarters: the sun-drenched, hundred-thousand-square-foot Discovery Center. Here Tyson's research and development staff of 160 work with global clientele to develop new protein products, test new protein flavor profiles, and conduct consumer research.

A giant sculpture of a fork loomed above the Discovery Center, along with a titanic frying pan that held gargantuan slices of ceramic bacon. From each cubicle divider hung shiny color photographs of beef enchiladas, chicken breasts, and, of course, pepperoni pizza. As far as the eye could see stretched an endless series of conference rooms, packaging labs, and kitchen after kitchen outfitted with video cameras, one-way mirrors, and an impressive collection of webcast paraphernalia. Food technologists, certified culinary scientists, and research and development wonks milled around the premises, contemplating shredded beef at nine o'clock in the morning. The place smelled like a barbecue.

I met with Brian Hafley, a Tyson food technologist with a PhD in pepperoni. Actually, Hafley wrote his food science dissertation on high-tech meat thermometers. But two of his great-grandfathers had been sausage makers, and now, after fifteen years in the business, Hafley has become a wiener master. "I couldn't fight destiny," he said.

Hafley guided me through an academic exegesis on the nature of pepperoni sticks and slices, replete with digressions into such obscure corners of the business as moisture and acidity, lactic acid and sodium nitrite, hemicellulose, antioxidants, rancidity, rosemary, and oleoresin—the oil of paprika that gives pepperoni its signature dried pumpkin–orange color. Then came Hafley's pepperoni PowerPoint presentation, and I learned that pepperoni dates back to ancient Rome. Pepperoni is not actually cooked, but fermented and dried, and this fermenting and drying poses the immense challenge of the sausage. Hafley explained that drying the pepperoni takes up a lot of space and a great deal of time, which translates into real estate and rent.

Class dismissed; the moment had come to inspect the product. Hafley led me through a few test kitchens, past rethermalizers, ultravacs, and programmable cooking units with touch screens and scanner guns. We strode across concrete floors, past huge blenders and injectors and into a droning zone of Wonka-like metal tubing. From here, Hafley led me down some stairs to the stainless-steel pipes, tanks, conveyor belts, and multicolored hoses of Tyson's forty-thousand-square-foot pilot plant. We dressed in white smocks, donned hairnets, splashed through an antiseptic puddle to wash the soles of our shoes, and finally stepped onto the production floor.

Hafley pointed out the freezers, the blenders, and a table piled high with spring-locked metal ham molds. He was particularly proud of Tyson's "final grinder," which included a sophisticated bone elimination system. Then there was a million-dollar computerized water-jet knife, which could decide in its computer-knife brain which way to cut a chicken breast to maximize the yield of chicken meat. Everywhere I looked I was surrounded by protein—beef extruding from grinders onto vast platters, pork hanging from hooks—and not only beef and pork but all the thrumming technologies of beef, pork, and poultry, all the ways human beings had learned to cook and flavor and test and sell the flesh of animals.

Eventually, Hafley unbolted and slid open a thick steel door, and we entered a refrigerated vault. In the dim light hung his latest creation, a hundred-pound batch of day-old pepperoni that gently swayed against the auto-timed sprays of a humidity nozzle. I had reached the cold core of the Meatrix.

Hafley spoke in hushed tones, as though too much human voice might disturb the infant sausages. The maturing pepperoni, Hafley whispered, was kept under constant computerized surveillance. Any unexpected change in temperature or humidity would sound an alarm, for a single ruined batch would set his research back weeks, if not months.

Hafley dared not be too optimistic. A lot could go wrong with a stick of pepperoni. But given final approval from Tyson's higher-ups, his beloved sausage just might get to enter mass production. Then his pepperoni would no longer cure in the side fridge of a basement, but within a capacious, three-story temperature- and humidity-controlled smokehouse. The production process would take up to a month, after which Tyson machines would bulk-slice the lot, seal the rounds in enormous plastic bags, and load the product into tremendous cardboard boxes that once crammed with pepperoni came in at just under a ton. "We can't afford to go wrong," Hafley said. "We have too much invested in pepperoni."

We headed back to the test kitchens, where a surprise awaited: five bubbling-from-the-oven Tyson's pepperoni pizzas. I confess that over the years I have enjoyed more than my fair share of pepperoni pizza, and these looked tremendous.

But before we ate, Hafley asked that I inspect the pepperoni's particle definition and the mozzarella's uncanny uniformity of melt—the technical perfection of the product. I could not help but admire the ingenious summation of disparate global commodities that had congealed into this emblem of world culture: a take-out pizza.

Eventually I placed a call to Domino's CEO J. Patrick Doyle and asked him to respond to the allegation that take-out pizza was not providing inexpensive, delicious, and healthy food to the world as much as it was increasing the planet's misery. He asked me to tell him how I had come to such a conclusion, so I outlined all I had learned about the process tomato, Big Dairy, and the intensive meat complex. Doyle was unperturbed. "The fact that our brand has global scale is the source of the question," he said. "But all our stores are owned locally, and we reinvest in local markets just like any other locally owned and operated business. We employ locally, we source locally, and we are absolutely a part of the community."

I was about to take Doyle up on his claims about local sourcing. Was his Malaysian pizza as locally sourced as his Paradise Tomato Kitchens pizza sauce, which someone had to truck from California to Detroit? And what about the cheese from Denver? And the pepperoni from Arkansas? But I decided not to quibble over food miles and long-distance supply chains just as the CEO was inviting me to corporate headquarters.

•   •   •

I had not grasped all the forces that lay behind the global explosion of pizza, so before I visited Domino's corporate headquarters I drove up to Ithaca, New York, to talk to Philip McMichael, a professor of development sociology at Cornell who has for many years been one of the principal philosophical foes of transnational food.

Tony Weis, the Canadian professor who explained global meat to me, had been a student of McMichael's. Raj Patel, the food activist and best-selling author who exposed how global malnutrition and global obesity were two sides of the same coin, had also studied with McMichael. In fact, McMichael is one of the unheralded founders of the food movement, an academic famous within the circle of development sociology but whose name is hardly known outside the field.

I invited him to dinner at the Moosewood, the restaurant collective that not only helped popularize American locavorism but canonized the broccoli, cheese, and brown rice casserole. Moosewood was one of the first spots in this country where countercultural cuisine had declared war against agribusiness, and the vegetarian menu still reflects the ecological and social ideals of the late 1960s. I figured that the Moosewood would be a fitting spot to discuss global pizza.

McMichael has a taste for organic beer and the intricacies of international trade policy, so over an order of guacamole and chips the professor outlined the history of corporate food production and global distribution. He described how twentieth-century agriculture's emphasis on mass production, its ever increasing reliance on industrial fossil fuels, and its relentless search for the most rapidly expanding overseas markets led to what is, in his opinion, nothing less than a new world order. He called it the "food regime."

Since agribusiness has played a central role in the construction of the global economy, the food regime has become one of the most powerful forces on the planet. Yet most of Earth's affluent billion remain oblivious to the food regime's impact and significance. When the cupboard lacks chips and the fridge lacks beer, we hop in the car and drive to the grocery store. Or if we simply want food to appear on the table, we order a pizza.

Such is not the case throughout most of the world. McMichael explained that as the percentage of the world's population that lives in cities increases, the percentage of people able to produce their own food decreases. Hundreds of millions of small-scale farmers have abandoned their rural livelihoods and migrated to the urban ghettoes of cities like Jakarta, Indonesia (population 24.9 million); Dhaka, Bangladesh (25 million); and Karachi, Pakistan (26.5 million). And the largest human migration in history is not about to stop. Within thirty years, the global slums will have to absorb yet another billion bankrupt and uneducated former farmers, the majority of whom will not be able to find employment—and will end up worse than they were before.

"Europe and America protect their farming with massive subsidies and insist the global south open up to their food," McMichael observed. "The irony is that the small farmers being pushed off the land *feed the majority of the world's population.*"

Big tomato kills small tomato. The more milk, the less milk. And now, in the name of mass food production, there would be less food for the masses.

●   ●   ●

Ann Arbor, Michigan, is the home of the white-fenced, low-slung, American-flag-bedecked, modernist headquarters of Domino's Pizza. The lobby is immense. One endless stretch presents an extensive, museum-style exhibit of the company's story, the historical highlights marked by articles clipped from Domino's internal news arm, the *Pepperoni Press*. There was an original "Noid" from the ad campaign of 1986 and a Domino's-branded NASCAR Toyota parked in the middle of the floor. Next to the car stood a very large trophy. Every year, a silver cup is awarded to the Domino's employee who makes the fastest pizza. Current championship time: three entire pizzas in thirty seconds. "Our business is all about making it quick," said my old friend from the distribution center, Chris Brandon.

Next to the trophy sat another Domino's Pizza icon, the oversized, infamous "man cave" couch. It was a black leather number with two built-in flat-screen televisions, a built-in DVD player, assorted minifridges, XBoxes, MP3 players, and an XM radio. In the man cave, a take-out pizza is as indispensable as the football game and the beer, and it implies much more than food. The take-out pizza has become a central element of American middle-class maledom.

Past the lobby, a great circular staircase snaked around a glass-enclosed space known locally as the Pizza Theater. Every new Domino's employee, from marketing assistant to CEO, must spend four days in this glass-walled lyceum, learning to take phone orders, compile pies, and deploy product throughout the Domino's corporate campus.

"It was fabulous," CEO Doyle said of his time at pizza school. "There is nothing as satisfying as making a great-looking pizza and doing it relatively quickly, and getting it delivered to a customer and having him be pleased with the experience."

I observed future Domino's franchise owners as they toiled next to the 465-degree-Fahrenheit impingement oven, a piece of ingenious cooking technology that forces superheated air above and below a pizza-carrying conveyor belt. Two of the trainees were from Chile, one from Indonesia. "We're introducing the product to people who have never had it before," said Brandon.

Lunch orders phoned and e-mailed in from other floors of the building had began to pop up on screens, and Kenji, Ghanem, and Nandidi bustled from the computers to the cutting station and back. I stood out of harm's way and marveled at the clear plastic trays of ingredients that could produce eighty-eight million different pizzas, as Brandon proudly noted—or, at the very least, eighty-eight million pseudo-varieties of the industrialized world's single pie.

In the middle of the action stood the master pizza maker, Sam Fauser. When he was a child, his ambition had been to work for the Ford Motor Company, but the assembly line he now commanded was, in his opinion, even better. "I live the dream every day," he said. I asked Fauser if it wasn't a challenge to work with people from all over the world, from the widest variety of backgrounds and cultures. "We all speak a common language," he said. "The pizza language."

I asked him what he made of the fact that the global pizza industry was growing at an annual rate of 40 percent, that Tyson Foods produces enough pepperoni slices each year to cover twenty-three thousand acres, and that Americans eat 350 slices of pizza every second. From where we stood in the glass-walled Pizza Theater, it looked as though assembly-line pizza was helping to feed the world. Fauser nodded. "When I was a kid, pizza was a treat," he said. "Now it's a staple." At which point Fauser grabbed a pepperoni pizza and sliced and boxed it in less than five seconds, and delivered it into my hands.

My little visit to Domino's world headquarters was coming to a close, but with all the good-byes and thank-yous, I didn't settle down to the pepperoni pie until half an hour later. Never before had I tasted a Domino's pizza, but now I downed one slice after another as globs of chemical umami swirled over my tongue. The crunch and the goo were addictive, unlike any other pizza I had ever eaten or would ever eat again. The pizza was sweet, salty, and buttery—all at the same time. When I didn't want another slice, I still wanted another slice.

When you manufacture pizza like any other widget, the only way to make it delicious is to add the contents of that "goody bag" to the industrial soy crush, the commodity wheat, the AB2 tomatoes, the easy-freeze and easy-melt mozzarella, and Tyson's dry cured protein. The secret contents of the goody bag are really not so secret: it's mostly salt and sugar. And Jimmy Leprino's patented cheese delivers the fat. Three slices of global pizza bring you near your daily caloric limit and give you more salt, sugar, and fat than recommended—and not much else. Of course, nutrition is one thing, market share another.

And as I stood and wolfed down slice after slice, a savage holler welled up from the depths of the glass lobby. "Sell more pizza!" clamored the budding globalists. "Have more fun!" This was the Domino's cheer, explained Brandon. "You hear that quite a bit."

Domino's Pizza was a great step forward in the history of eating, I told Brandon. But when it came to bringing inexpensive, delicious, and healthy food to everyone on Earth, Domino's delivered too many negatives. At the end of the day, Big Pizza was unsustainable.

"We're in the midst of celebrating our fiftieth year," said Brandon. "If that's not sustainable, what is?"

3

The Measure
of All Things

There is a world peasant movement, and it is called La
Via Campesina. Founded in the last decade of the
twentieth century, La Via Campesina defends family
farms, promotes sustainable food production, and generally
avoids take-out pizza.

Recently, the world peasant movement protested the transnational food producers' habit of burning down immense
tracts of Earth's forests and jungles in order to blanket the
land with commodity grains that could be crushed into commodity oils or fed to commodity chicken or beef. La Via
Campesina asserted that turning great swaths of the planet

into smoldering piles of ashes was not good for native flora and fauna, not to mention the lives and livelihoods of the people who had been living there. The practice, the group said, was unsustainable.

The world peasant movement pointed out that more than 60 percent of the people on the planet have come to rely on a total of four crop species: corn, rice, soy, and wheat. If any one of these crops were to fail because of drought or disease, disaster would surely follow. Less monoculture and more agroecological farming, reasoned La Via Campesina, would create more inexpensive, healthy, and delicious food for more people on Earth. Biodiversity is better than deforestation.

The argument seemed straightforward enough, but no one could understand it—at least, no one in any position to do anything about it. For La Via Campesina had not translated its reasoning about food into the new language of food. Of course, there might have been a good reason for this oversight. Perhaps La Via Campesina had not translated its reasoning about food into the new language of food because it did not know there *was* a new language of food.

Perhaps the world peasant movement had not heard of the Economics of Ecosystems and Biodiversity (TEEB), an international initiative hosted by the U.N. Environment Program and supported by the European Commission, Germany, the United Kingdom, the Netherlands, Norway, Sweden, and Japan. The idea behind TEEB is that biodiversity has cash value, and the goal is to calculate the cost of ecosystem degradation down to the last trillion dollars, riyals, or yuan—the language that corporations and governments understand.

The conversion of ecological ideas into economic terms has become necessary, declared TEEB's mission statement, because "modern society's predominant focus on market-delivered components of well-being, and our almost total dependence on market prices to indicate value, means that we generally do not measure or manage economic values exchanged other than through markets."

In order to possess meaning, biodiversity had to be measured and managed. For biodiversity, like every other component of industrial production and corporate well-being, had to fit on a ledger. Biodiversity had to be translated into a new language. And TEEB had begun to provide some of the tools necessary to render the Earth, the sun, and the rain into a *market-delivered component*.

Unfortunately, in their haste to halt the defoliation of the planet, the world peasant movement had neglected to make its claim about biodiversity into a claim about a market-delivered component. Perhaps La Via Campesina did not see a direct correspondence between the glories of nature and the glories of the market. Perhaps it rejected the belief that biodiversity must be translated into economic terms. No matter. The peasants did not speak the new language of sustainability, so no one heard them.

La Via Campesina is not the only group that has this problem. Many of us do not believe we need a quotient or a sum to be convinced that the world requires biodiversity more than monoculture, that we need small farmers more than Big Pizza and agroecology more than agribusiness. It might be an overstatement to call this conflict a war or to say we choose sides every time we buy anything at the grocery store. We simply have a hunch that despite the protests of Chris Brandon and Domino's Pizza, industrial agriculture is radically unsustainable.

Soon the days of hunches may be gone. Mathematical proofs are percolating, proofs not to be denied by those who mistake spreadsheets for food.

Through the 1780s and the 1790s, an English scholar named Thomas Malthus observed that the accelerating technologies of the Industrial Revolution had lured an ever growing number of impoverished men and women to London and other urban centers. In 1798 he published *An Essay on the Principle of Population*, in which he predicted that population growth would eventually outpace food production and that as a result, multitudes of people—poor urban dwellers, to be specific—were destined to lack healthy and inexpensive (forget about delicious) food and die.

Ever since the publication of Malthus's infamous *Essay*, the question of the world's food supply has hinged on the question of sustainability, and the question of sustainability has hinged on the limits of growth. The argument Malthus began continues. On one side are those who perceive that every new generation brings more people to the planet, but along with an ever growing population comes an ever increasing food supply. As scientists search for ways to draw the most from seed and soil, business executives believe that technical innovations will extend indefinitely. In other words, the more people there are on Earth, the more people the earth will be able to feed. The limits of growth have not been reached.

On the other side of the argument are those who believe that a billion hungry people means that the catastrophe Malthus foresaw is already here, even if the industrial food system refuses to admit it. This side watches as growing populations in the developing world adopt industrialized diets that make them unhealthy and deplete the world's resources. They see starvation everywhere else. They believe the limits of growth *have* been reached.

Who is right? The answers are not at all obvious. But the dispute comes down to the question of sustainability.

Chris Brandon and Domino's Pizza are not alone in their view of sustainability. Many people will tell you that large-scale agriculture is our only hope to feed the world, that small farmers should leave food to the big guys and figure out a way to join the urban economy, that conventional agriculture is more cost-effective than organic agriculture, and that the only road to a sustainable future leaves antiquated ways behind. Sorting out the truth is harder than it sounds, for much like biodiversity, sustainability does not easily fall into quantifiable terms. Still, the growing ranks of eco-number crunchers persist in their conviction that sustainability can be counted. They also believe that the discovery of this mathematical measure would be the greatest intellectual, social, and scientific achievement of our generation.

One day we may know how much of Earth's energy and resources are embodied in every bite and every sip. One day we may be able to calculate a measurement that we might call a *sustainability unit*. And whatever that sustainability unit may be, the measurement will allow us to compare the amount of energy and resources necessary to produce a plastic bottle of Lipton tea from a vending machine to the number of sustainability units necessary to produce a ceramic cup of steaming Bigelow mint tea with honey and two tablespoons of 2 percent organic milk.

Then we will know the relative sustainability values (whatever they may be) not only of hot and cold tea but also of an order of french fries, a plate of spaghetti and meatballs, a grilled cheese sandwich, a scrambled egg, a Domino's pizza, or cassava root unearthed in Tanzania. Then we will be able to calculate production and consumption in a new way and know precisely how much healthy and delicious food the world can generate—of what kind, for how long, and for how many people. On that day sustainability will become hard science, and we will possess the measure of all things.

Such measurements will open up a potentially shattering body of knowledge. As a result, a great deal of anxiety and obsession cloud the infant field of sustainability studies. No surprise, then, that as we move into the third millennium of the Common Era, sustainability has been embraced by those whose business is not science, economics, demographics, farming, or philosophy. Sustainability has become the first great marketing tool of the twenty-first century. There's a lot of money in it.

"We are faced with two possible futures," said Harriet Friedmann, a professor of geography and planning at the University of Toronto. "One is a diversity of crops, of cultures, and of cuisines that can inhabit ecosystems sustainably and produce healthy food for urban centers. The other is long-distance food from nowhere, monocultural systems that aren't sustainable, and simplified diets, especially for the poor. Global pizza typifies the second option."

Over those organic beers at the Moosewood, Philip McMichael had suggested I put in a call to Friedmann, his colleague and collaborator. Friedmann has written about sustainable food systems, sustainable farming, sustainable development, and sustainable alternatives to the corporate strategies of transnational food producers. It was Friedmann who had coined the term *food regime*, the view of modern history that places the practices of the agro-industrial complex at the center of unsustainable world economics and global politics.

Friedmann condemned Domino's, Pizza Hut, and Little Caesars. But I became skeptical when she told me there were two possible futures, because I suspected there were thousands of possible futures. Two possible anythings make me uneasy. Just when you're about to choose one or the other, a third reality creeps in and changes the ball game. Friedmann's vision of sustainable farming by savvy ruralists and sustainable eating by affluent urban dwellers sounded like a great idea, but I didn't know if it could really provide healthy and delicious food for everyone on Earth.

"The only sustainable form of production is to have farmers become ecosystem managers as well as producers," she continued. "What we need to do is renew farming in the countryside so that it reconnects with the crops, animals, cheeses, and meats that are now appropriate for the kinds of cuisines that are evolving in the cities, a farming system related to a cuisine that is sustainable. All our measures of efficiency have measured labor efficiency, so we are proud that tiny quantities of people can produce so much rice or pork. And while we charge along in this unsustainable direction, something completely new is trying to emerge."

I wanted to believe in a straightforward conflict between diversity and monoculture, health and sickness, sustainability and unsustainability, the old and the new, and evil corporations and noble farmers, but Friedmann was using the word *sustainable* as though everybody already knew what it meant. The more I thought about healthy and affordable food for everyone, the less I thought about boxes of pepperoni pizzas metastasizing across the continents; the less I thought about green markets, heirloom vegetables, and affluent city dwellers; and the more I thought about basic elements like wheat, milk, and tomatoes. On the surface, there is nothing apocalyptic about a banana, a potato, or a hunk of mozzarella. But what if each item carried within itself a secret quotient of economic, environmental, political, and social ruin? Those numbers would add up to the true price of our daily bread.

Once food had been transformed into this new language, the agribusiness number crunchers could pinpoint problems. They could assess and evaluate every social, environmental, and political point on the graph. Then, armed with data, histograms, and regressions, they could begin to manage what had been measured and improve it.

Wouldn't such a purely numerical measure of sustainability constitute the truth that lay behind our food: organic, industrial, and everything in between? For this measure of all things would not be visionary, political, or social. It would be scientific and statistical. But at this point my contemplations reached a troubling conclusion: After every conceivable quanta of sustainability had been collected, down to the last grain of rice and drop of water, what if Chris Brandon and J. Patrick Doyle were right and Harriet Friedmann, Tony Weis, and Philip McMichael were wrong? What if the food regime was, in fact, *sustainable*?

Given a strictly scientific set of conclusions based on quantified sustainability measurements, it would be impossible to lay the blame for global misery at the feet of transnational agribusiness. In that case, I would be making a big mistake. It was not the most *gigantic* food producers and distributors I should be trailing in my search for inexpensive, healthy, and delicious food for everyone, but the most *efficient* food producers—and not just in terms of labor and output but in as complete and totalized a fashion as possible.

That was how I came to the tomato farm run by Frank Muller and his two brothers in Yolo County, California. The Muller megafarm was famous throughout the Sacramento Valley. People said it was the most efficient operation of its kind in California—and possibly the world. Muller, people said, was a new breed of profit-oriented, information-savvy, ultra-efficient, sustainable farmer.

I arrived around noon on a clear spring day, walked along the mud-caked fringe of Muller farmland, and tried in vain to make out the profiles of a quarter of a million baby tomato plants. It was hard to believe that in just a few months this perfect rectangle of endless muck would burst into three million pounds of ripe red fruit, and it was even stranger to consider that somehow this vast monoculture might lead the world toward agricultural sustainability—particularly considering that not one of the plants in this field was organic, heirloom, or pesticide-free. But the Muller farm had been advertised as a peek into the future of agritechnology. The key around here was measurement, and Muller was obsessive about what went into and came out of his business. "When I see my fields, I see a canvas," he said.

Muller and his brothers are the sons of Swiss immigrants who settled in California less than half a century ago, and even though they do cultivate a few organic fruits and vegetables here and there, when it comes to the health and well-being of their cash crop, process tomatoes, the brothers rely on conventional farming methods. "If you're not organic, it doesn't mean you're bad," Muller said. Still, the notion of the world's megafarms leading the way to global sustainability and inexpensive, delicious, healthy food for all would chill the hearts of farm-to-table activists like Dan Barber and Alice Waters and their legions of followers. The very idea opposes the philosophy and politics of the slow-food movement, the food justice movement, the good-food movement, the edible movement, the grass-fed movement, the organic movement, the locavore movement, the food sovereignty movement, the food-first movement, and the global peasant movement led by La Via Campesina.

Muller and his brothers farm 219 mammoth tracts of land in the Sacramento Valley. Last year, the brothers sold sixty thousand tons of their tomato harvest to transnational food giant Unilever, which subsequently processed the lot into bottles of Ragú's Cheesy, Chunky, and Robusto spaghetti sauces.

Unilever, people told me, is a global leader in sustainable agriculture. And Unilever was not the only multinational corporation searching for quantifiable measures of sustainability. Over the past several years, some of the world's mightiest and most profitable tomato syndicates—including Del Monte and Heinz, along with Unilever—have allied themselves with a small, relatively unknown, and extraordinarily ambitious consortium called the Stewardship Index for Specialty Crops.

Let's assume for a moment that the tomatocrats are right: the only problem with industrial agriculture is that the system has yet to reach its potential, and conventional farming has not yet truly realized itself. Let's assume that the naysayers in the food movement are no different from the Luddites who would argue that a handwritten letter is better than an e-mail, newspaper ink on your hands is better than a Kindle or a Nook, and baseball was better before strict training regimens and complicated statistics. Let's assume that given the opportunity and incentive, industrial agriculture will inevitably become more productive, efficient, sophisticated, and sustainable. The business simply needs more time to mature and innovate—broken eggs and omelets and all that. If these assumptions are correct, the future of food begins with the Stewardship Index for Specialty Crops.

In 2008, the Stewardship Index for Specialty Crops began to bring together many of those who share a stake in industrial agriculture, be they farmers, packagers, retailers, environmentalists, or food activists. The first goal of the consortium was to get all of these stakeholders to agree on what, exactly, everyone ought to measure in order to understand and gauge the total effect of the seed-to-shelf life cycle of any produce-based product, from frozen french fries to canned almonds to bottled pasta sauce. The Stewardship Index for Specialty Crops split its sustainability index project into working committees that include representatives from food giants such as Bayer CropScience, Cisco, General Mills, PepsiCo, Sodexo, and Walmart; trade groups such as the Western Growers Association and the National Potato Council; and numerous environmental organizations and flocks of academics—from the University of California at Berkeley, Stanford University, Yale University, and the University of Arkansas's Sam M. Walton College of Business.

The Stewardship Index for Specialty Crops calls its proposed yardsticks *sustainability metrics*, and the hope is that once all of the stakeholders in the food business can translate sustainability into numbers, they will be able to compare and contrast their sustainability scores with those of their industry peers, eliminate excesses, and grow more food with less environmental impact. The logic is fairly straightforward: sustainability aligns with efficiency, and the elimination of any size, shape, or form of wasted resource will save the world's largest and smallest companies untold dollars, euros, pounds, riyals, and yuan. The earth will produce the most food possible for as long as possible. Stewardship of the environment and feeding everyone on the planet will align with the profit motive, and sustainability metrics will become the lingua franca of the staunch capitalist, the radical environmentalist, the food activist, and everyone in between. At least that's the idea.

Jeff Dlott is the founder, CEO, and chairman of the board of SureHarvest, a company that sells sustainability strategies, sustainability consulting services, and sustainability management software. "We make sustainability quantifiable, practical, and profitable," says the SureHarvest website. What could be better than saving Earth and making money at the same time? "My job is to make farmers spend less to make your products," Dlott told me. "But what we really get paid for is technical work, crunching numbers, graphics, and building software systems."

It occurred to me that in the future, the food supply chain, cash flow, and environmental impact may be virtually indistinguishable. In fact, one of SureHarvest's long-term goals has been to merge money and ecology into a single new product for the food industry, a medium of exchange SureHarvest calls *sustainability currency*.

Dlott is the founder of many things. He founded SureHarvest, and he cofounded the Stewardship Index for Specialty
Crops. In addition to all of that founding, Dlott has been
contributing to the world's largest retailer's attempt to design
its own sustainability index. Dlott has been working with
Walmart. Why, I asked him, had so many big players in the
food business all decided at the same time to push so hard to
measure and manage sustainability? He explained that in the
wake of the nation's 2006 E. coli scare, in which three people died from tainted lettuce, the West Coast's leafy greens
business had been forced to adopt strict food safety agendas.
"Health scares were already costing the growers and processors extra money to meet new sets of protocols," said Dlott.
"What could they do to protect themselves?"

I didn't know what to say. It had not occurred to me that
sustainability might be a defensive maneuver on the part of
the food industry. But as it turned out, by the end of the first
decade of the twenty-first century, a number of agritech gurus
in the San Francisco Bay Area had already begun to suspect
that after food safety, the next great regulatory threat to their
business model would center on sustainability. And rather
than sit and wait for sustainability regulations to be forced on
them, a number of farmers, processors, and retailers decided
to take the offensive and define *sustainable* for themselves.
"If we don't do it," Dlott told me, "it's going to get done to us."

The idea of regulating the regulators before they regulate
you is a time-honored tradition and has earned its own economic catchphrase: *market capture*. As a matter of course,
the group that will be most affected by outside regulation will
spend a great deal of time, energy, and resources shaping the
upcoming regulations to fit its own wants and needs. The result:
Those who are about to be regulated "capture" the "market" in

their own regulation. Consider the motion picture ratings system, which the motion picture industry defines for itself. Now
imagine motion picture ratings as an agricultural sustainability
rating system that agriculture has defined for itself.

Now imagine Walmart in charge of that system.

For Dlott and his visionary cohorts were not alone in their
conviction that agriculture was about to face a sustainability
challenge and that they had better preempt it. A group called
Scientific Certification Systems had already begun to draft a
national standard for sustainable agriculture, a product that the
group could offer alongside its sustainable aquaculture certification, its sustainable seafood certification, its Forest Stewardship
Council certification, and a host of other eco-branding products.

Then there was the American National Standards Institute, a group that had previously set guidelines and criteria
for acoustical devices, construction equipment, nanotechnol-
ogy, and nuclear energy and was now attempting to quantify
sustainability. Malthus would have been proud. Hordes of
corporations and consortiums had begun to work the limits-
to-growth gig he had inaugurated two centuries before, companies like New Zealand's Greentick, Los Angeles's Green
Globe, and a media group that called itself GreenBiz.

Malthus had posed a ruthless question: Could agricultural
growth keep pace with population growth? The question
was simple, but the answer was complicated. And in the last
decade, our ideas of sustainability have grown ever more
intricate, to the point that each of the organizations and
institutes in the burgeoning sustainability-metric business
possess a different notion of what sustainability means and
how it might be measured. And since no one can define the
standard of sustainability because sustainability has yet to be

translated into a quantifiable measurement, the first company to succeed in disseminating its equations would, for all intents and purposes, own the standard.

The problem of defining something before it exists has introduced yet another series of complications. For it is one thing to own a standard, another to sell it. And as it turns out, the appeal of a sustainability standard depends in no small part on the strictness of that standard—in particular, whether the proposed sustainability regulations would be more or less stringent than the regulations that govern organic food.

Dlott explained that even though the demand for organic food is steadily growing, organic remains a niche market, accounting for less than 1 percent of the total U.S. agricultural output. And to say that the standard for sustainability would be the organic standard plus more, well, the national corn growers and the national wheat growers—the megafarmers and the megafood producers—they were not going to buy a sustainability standard like that.

When we focus on feeding everyone, environmentalism becomes a sticky subject. There are human needs and there are the ecosystem's needs, and they are not always the same. Or so it seems. But this new idea, *quantified sustainability*, looked as though it could bridge the gap. Everything would change if the fates of megafood producers were identical with the fate of the Earth.

Then again, none of the competing sustainability measures and indexes out there were about to guarantee for the future of our planet what Bayer CropScience, Cisco, Dow, General

Mills, Kraft, PepsiCo, Nestlé, Sodexo, and Walmart wanted to guarantee for themselves, which was long-term prosperity. The transnationals wanted to define sustainability in their own language. They wanted to capture the market.

And that was where the Stewardship Index for Specialty Crops had something new to offer, something its competitors in the sustainability business lacked. The Stewardship Index, created by the farmers, the food processors, and the retailers, found an ally that in the past had eluded all of them: the environmental activists.

The food producers discovered an unexpected and welcome comrade in Jonathan Kaplan, a senior policy specialist at the Natural Resources Defense Council (NRDC), an international nonprofit organization with an annual operating income of more than ninety-nine million dollars and hundreds of lawyers on staff. The NRDC's mission statement calls for "a new way of life for humankind, one that can be sustained indefinitely without fouling or depleting the resources that support all life on earth." The *New York Times* has called the NRDC "one of the nation's most powerful environmental groups."

Like most reasonable people, Kaplan realized that for the sake of the planet and everyone on it, agriculture must become more sustainable. But organic agriculture, Kaplan understood, was not the most inclusive approach to saving the world. He knew the production statistics. He understood that an organic-style standard for sustainable agriculture would not effect the vast changes he envisioned, because organic would never be accepted as a standard by those who could effect such changes.

Environmental activists, reasoned Kaplan, had to focus on the practices of the other 99 percent of agricultural production, which meant the practices of conventional farmers. The kind of sustainability index that could be embraced by conventional farmers might not be perfect, but it would provide environmentalists with a new window into the conventions of agribusiness, along with the possibility of changing those conventions somewhere down the line. This was an astonishing admission from an environmentalist: local and organic was nice, but it was not the answer.

Kaplan realized that the only kind of sustainability a transnational could understand would be sustainability translated into a market-delivered component, sustainability that could fit on a spreadsheet. "This index is like an accounting system for sustainable agriculture and sustainable food production," Kaplan told me. "Accountants have all kinds of metrics—price-to-earnings ratios, protocols for evaluating a company's financial health—but we don't really have anything like that for sustainability."

Unlike La Via Campesina, Kaplan was learning the new language of food. "The lowest performers in the system are the ones we most need to step up and improve their practices," he said. "We want to get the low-hanging fruit, and we're going to get at that when we start measuring and comparing."

Kaplan's pragmatic perceptions brought the NRDC into the Stewardship Index fold, and other environmental powerhouses followed. The Organic Center, a research institute focused on the science of organic food and organic farming, joined the indexing effort to quantify sustainable agriculture, and so did the Sierra Club and the World Wildlife Fund. Under the aegis of the Stewardship Index for Specialty Crops, environmental organizations were offering to support agribusiness in its efforts to measure all that was possible to measure—and thereby transform the production of food into a vast store of analyzable data.

After Kaplan, Dlott, and a few other food industry experts and lobbyists founded the Stewardship Index for Specialty Crops, one of their first jobs was to form committees that could conceptualize sustainability measurements for every possible effect the production of food might have on air quality, soil quality, water quality, biodiversity, greenhouse gases, and energy use. That was a lot to conceptualize, and the nature of the exercise led to an unanticipated problem: indexed food, it turned out, was not at all like the real thing.

Along with Kaplan and Dlott, the founders of the Stewardship Index included Hank Giclas, the head of strategic planning for a trade association called Western Growers, whose three thousand members grow, pack, and ship 70 percent of the fruit and nuts in Arizona and California. Western Growers is an important force in U.S. agriculture, and Giclas happens to be a very smart man. He was among the first to perceive that agriculture's sustainability question was about to become a business liability and that sooner or later his industry would be held accountable for who knew how many sins of unsustainability.

Giclas perceived yet another factor in the equation: the matter of sustainability as it pertained to information. He knew that the Stewardship Index was about to be the recipient of a mother lode of data about food, and he anticipated the challenge of keeping all that data confidential. He understood that keeping all of the food data secret was going to be a more immediate problem for the Stewardship Index than the problem of transforming all of it into some sort of unit measurement of sustainability. "How we protect and share data is going to be the linchpin issue for the long-term viability and short-term success of the Stewardship Index," Giclas told me by phone from his office at Western Growers. "Let's talk about nitrogen input," he continued, using the general term for the synthetic fertilizers that power conventional agriculture. "When applied, what application methods, how much is applied—these are considered production secrets. You're going to have a hesitancy on the part of some folks to share that specificity of data, because that's their competitive advantage."

Measuring sustainability was fine as long as no one ever knew *how* you measured it or measured up. And if the complications of nitrogen fertilizer were such that they had to remain confidential, the intricacies of water usage were nearly impossible for anyone outside the business to comprehend. So they had to be kept secret, too.

Giclas explained that unlike the Muller brothers and their drip irrigation–obsessed megafarm, many of his growers did not possess the great good fortune of residing in Yolo County, one of the most water-rich agricultural regions in the country. If these less aquatically blessed farmers were to reveal how much water their process tomatoes required (if, in fact, they collected such data or even had the capacity to collect such data), their consumption of nonlocal water would immediately become apparent. If made public, the water-import data—water miles, as it were—might drive eco-minded consumers away from their products.

Since the supposed power of the Stewardship Index measurements would be to make clear what had always been obscure about our food, these measurements would possess implications that reached far beyond the farmers' use of locally sourced water or water pumped in from the Rocky Mountains. American consumers spend more than a trillion dollars a year on food. What would happen to the potato industry if water, nitrogen, diesel, and greenhouse gas measurements were to reveal that in terms of environmental sustainability units (whatever they might be), a french fry cost ten to twenty times more than, say, an onion ring? If we really want the world's supply of inexpensive and delicious food to last, should we give up french fries? Not a trivial issue, by any account.

Giclas knew what his growers knew: a display of unsustainable numbers would be their downfall. So the Stewardship Index for Specialty Crops will not release any such data.

4

What's New
for Dinner

I bounced around the front seat of Frank Muller's pickup truck as he pushed it to seventy miles an hour down the rutted back roads of Yolo County. Muller floored the accelerator past tracts of garlic and onions, walnut trees, almond trees, and fields of winter wheat, and as he hit ever more ridiculous speeds he took a hand off the steering wheel to point out the cover crops: vetch (a legume), bell beans, winter peas, and buffer strips of triticale (a grain that is a hybrid of wheat and rye), all of which increase the soil's biodiversity and organic matter while reducing erosion. Cover crops are essential to agroecological attempts at sustainability, Muller explained. They reduce the need for synthetic fertilizers.

As Muller careened across Cache Creek, he described the geography of his farmland, which lies between California's coastal range and the four-hundred-mile-long Sierra Nevada. "We're in a big bowl," he said. "It's an amazing water area." On the plains of California's fertile crescent, Muller and his brothers cultivate sunflowers, bell peppers, jalapeños, and the yellow wax peppers that adorn the top of Subway sandwiches. The Mullers sell their wine grapes to makers of cabernet, chardonnay, sauvignon blanc, and Syrah. But most of all, they raise process tomatoes—the kind that sit atop pizzas and pour from jars of Ragú.

Muller parked his truck next to his barns, climbed out of the driver's seat, slammed the door, pulled out his iPhone, and checked the current wind speed, wind direction, and evapotranspiration rate, the sum of the velocities at which the sun draws moisture away from plants and soil. Taken together, this data would allow Muller to calculate how many hours a day he should run his irrigation system and at what rate. The farmer cut a picturesque figure aside his pickup, beneath the clear sky, as transfixed by his handheld device as any Wall Street banker.

On the Mullers' fields in Yolo County, the translation of agricultural customs into sustainability metrics had begun. Every decision Muller would make in his fields that day would be logged, archived, and analyzed back at the office. This wood-paneled space possessed a certain rustic charm— perhaps it was the John Deere clock, the cucumber wall calendar, or the bottle of Coon Creek olive oil decked out with a Best of Show ribbon from the 2008 Yolo County Fair. But the room revolved around Muller's double-screen computer, printers, fax machines, and shelves overloaded with dozens of thick black notebooks. Muller handed over one of those note- books, a volume titled *Cost Accounting 2008*, and I began to flip through a six-hundred-page report that listed every ele- ment that had gone into that year's tomato tonnage.

Muller monitors his soil's organic-matter level, moisture content, salinity, and pH, as well as its levels of nitrogen, phosphate, and potassium, and the ratio of magnesium to cal- cium. He counts the number of plant lice and tomato fruit worm larvae that live on each acre of his tomatoes. And by deploying hypercalibrated GPS devices that make the navi- gation system on your car's dashboard look like a Boy Scout compass, Muller can measure to the fraction of an inch the seemingly uncountable back-and-forths of his plows and hoes. Every slightest increase of efficiency means more sus- tainable farming, particularly when it comes to tractors. "Fuel is a good metric," he told me.

If Harriet Friedmann was right that we have only two options—high-tech industrial food or sustainable ecosystems— it was getting harder and harder to tell which side Muller was on. His measurements might have made old Thomas Malthus reconsider his insistence on the inevitability of starvation, for every data point supported an ever changing assessment of possible food production. And fortunately for Muller, all of that counting, accounting, management, and sustainability has cash value.

When fertilizer prices soared in 2008, Muller was able to offset the price increase by injecting 20 percent less chemi- cal nitrogen into his irrigation system than he had the previ- ous year, simply because his calculations indicated that his soil had enough nitrogen left over. The sustainability spread-sheet had allowed the ecosystem manager to relegate his costs as efficiently as if he had been an international currency trader protecting his stake in euros. If Muller's colleagues had made a similar accounting of their nitrogen and discovered that they too could have injected 20 percent less synthetic fertilizer into the ground, the savings across the country would have amounted to two and a half million tons of nitrogen fertilizer, or enough to grow thirty-three million acres of conventional tomatoes, and harvest as much as a billion more tons of tomatoes—which would be more than enough to top a startling number of piz-zas. Would you believe four trillion pizzas?

Most of the measurements in *Cost Accounting 2008* were devoted to water. Instead of using sprinklers (which generally miss their target) or furrows (notoriously inefficient), Muller again deployed GPS technology, this time to bury drip tape in the middle of each of his perfectly parallel rows of tomato vines. Installing GPS-guided irrigation drip tape can run a thousand dollars per acre, but the method generally pro-duces four tomatoes where there once were three, and since tomatoes equal cash, the money invested in water soon con-verts right back into money. And drip turns out to be a great measuring tool. Since the water goes straight to the roots, the calculation of a precise crop-per-drop measurement becomes possible.

On August 26 of the same year Muller discovered his crop-per-drop tomato measurement, CNBC.com reported that "water will eventually be traded like oil and gold and inves-tors should look to utilities right now for safe profit in volatile markets." Of course, not many farmers can say precisely how much water or how much fertilizer they use per acre of any of their crops. But as all agricultural inputs and outputs become indexed, farmers can begin to look, think, and act more like accountants. The transformation from dirt and rain to synthetic nitrogen and drip irrigation to the database may prove to be as great an innovation as tilling the soil was ten thousand years ago, around the time the science of accounting was first devised by ancient Egyptian agrocrats.

Still, as every accountant knows, any abstract symbol of value—be it a numerical representation of income, cash flow, or the plenitude of the earth—can hide as much as it reveals.

Behind the symbols lies the reality of the fresh-pack season: a hundred triple-shift days of picking, trucking, pureeing, and packing. Every year the marathon starts in mid-July and runs until mid-October, the three months when a summer's worth of California tomatoes must be condensed into a year's supply of pizza topping, salsa, and spaghetti sauce.

At the height of the season, Muller and his brothers spend their days and nights at the helms of harvesting machines, shepherding tens of thousands of ripe red tomatoes from their land to the double beds of sixteen-wheelers. Tomato-laden trailers pull out of the Muller megafarm at all hours and rumble down eighty miles of highway that cut through the greatest tomato-producing region in the world. Last year, the brothers sold their sixty thousand tons of tomatoes for nearly eighty dollars a ton. "You can tie the environmental and the economic together," Muller told me. "And we're close to this."

But once the tomatoes have left the ground, Muller's measurement is no longer water, diesel fuel, nitrogen fertilizer, soil pH, or pesticide. Once the tomatoes hit the sixteen-wheelers they begin to exhibit traits that make them appear less like food and more like market-delivered components. They began to behave like money.

A fleet of trucks carries the Mullers' red gold from the mud of Yolo County to the city streets of Stockton, California, home of the annual deep-fried asparagus competitive-eating world championships and of a Unilever tomato puree plant, the factory that processes every tomato that will become Ragú pasta sauce. To achieve maximum efficiency during the fresh-pack season and not waste a watt of electricity, a calorie of human labor, or a fraction of a gallon of gas, Unilever must manage a trucking operation that will deliver a constant stream of process tomatoes, enough to keep its stainless-steel tomato peelers at maximum capacity twenty-four hours a day, a hundred days running.

And as the trucks pull up to Unilever's barbed-wire enclosed parking lot and pass through the automatic gates, they leave Muller's spreadsheets and enter the data streams of the Anglo-Dutch transnational that sells not only Ragú but Ben and Jerry's, Bertolli, Hellman's, Knorr, Lipton, Slim-Fast, Skippy, and Q-tips.

I sat in the conference room of Unilever's tomato-smashing plant, enjoyed a PowerPoint presentation on process tomatoes, and stared at a wall plastered with Unilever tomato sauce measurements, known around the shop as the "daily KPIs" (key performance indicators). There were quite a few of them, ranging from the quantity of units produced to the sums of time and energy required to produce them to every trifling tomato leak or spill along the way. When it came to pasta sauce, sustainability was a matter of management, and the chief tomato manager at Unilever's Stockton plant wore blue jeans and cowboy boots. His name was Randy Rickert.

Rickert took me for a ride around the premises in his white pickup truck and explained that by the end of the fresh-pack season, the Stockton plant will have peeled, chopped, diced, pulped, boiled, condensed, and shipped half a million tons of raw tomatoes. We traced the labyrinth of pipes and vats that encircled an epic roller coaster of twisting conveyor belts, steel boilers, and cooling towers that marked Stockton's skyline. In a few weeks' time, everything here would be smeared red with tomato juice, tomato pulp, and tomato skin. The details of the operation looked complicated, but the general idea was basic: boil tomatoes.

Muller's tomatoes are 94 percent liquid, but they leave Unilever's plant reduced to 69 percent liquid. Why the evaporation stops at 69 percent remains a Ragú trade secret, but the logic behind the concentration is clear. Anything less than 69 percent would mean an excess expenditure of cooking time and effort, wattage, diesel, and money. Anything more than 69 percent liquid would increase transportation costs. Water is heavy, and half a million tons of tomato puree now had to be hauled by rail a few thousand miles east to Unilever's remanufacturing plant in Owensboro, Kentucky, where the water removed in Stockton would be returned by the banks of the Ohio River.

It might have made sense on the spreadsheet, but boiling off California water to make room for Ohio water made no sense to me. No doubt Unilever knew what it was doing, but I was beginning to question what the company meant by *sustainable*. What exactly did the word mean to them? And what, after all, was being made sustainable, the sauce or the price?

Still, almost everyone in the business hails Unilever as a leader in the new science. In 1997, the company piloted its first agricultural sustainability program, which tried to analyze the company's annual output of a hundred thousand boxes of frozen Bird's Eye peas. And after it had finished with frozen peas, Unilever attempted to analyze tea, spinach, and palm oil. These programs collected untold reams of data and stupefyingly vast fields of measurement, but despite years of work, Unilever's sustainability managers just could not manage to reduce all of the information into anything useful, such as a unit of sustainability. "In those early days it was impossible— we were measuring too much," said David Pendlington, Unilever's sustainable agriculture program coordinator. "We pretty much measured everything that moved, and we got killed by data collection."

The data had defeated Unilever's first attempts to quantify sustainability. The indexing had overwhelmed the food, and the failure forced the company to reassess its approach. The overwhelming vastness of tea and pea quanta had stopped up the pilot programs, but Unilever's solution was not a better computer or a new mode of analysis. Unilever simply decided to disregard all of the factors that had made the initial calculations too difficult to reduce to a unit. Sustainability could be only as sustainable as Unilever could understand.

So in 2001 Unilever turned its gaze toward tomatoes and asked that its contract growers in California report two numbers and only two numbers: nitrogen use and crop yield. During the next winter, Unilever aggregated and analyzed the fertilizer data and discovered that its least efficient growers were applying almost twice as much nitrogen to their fields as the most efficient but harvesting the same number of tomatoes. Here was a KPI for Ragú sauce worth noting. Growers were leaving money on the table—clearly not sustainable.

After the foray into fertilizer, Unilever asked for specific and verifiable measurements of water use. And soon thereafter, Unilever became convinced that it possessed a data set that exhibited optimal tomato-growing irrigation. That data set belonged to Frank Muller.

In two years, Unilever had uncovered two tomato-based sustainability benchmarks. At which point, Unilever's sustainable agriculture coordinator invited the biggest player in global food retail to come and see the results of the new, measurement-based model of sustainable agricultural production. And that was how Walmart came to Frank Muller's tomato farm.

Walmart, the biggest retailer of them all, could increase sales profits in two ways. First, it could sell more merchandise. Let's say more jars of pasta sauce. But at a certain point it becomes virtually impossible to sell more pasta sauce, because Walmart customers are already buying all the pasta sauce they need. What's more, Walmart cannot easily attract new customers who would presumably desire their own jars of sauce. Who out there would shop at Walmart who hasn't already heard of Walmart? Not very many people. So getting new people through the doors is as iffy as selling more sauce to customers who already buy sauce.

Second, Walmart could pay pasta sauce companies less for each bottle. And if Walmart could keep lowering the wholesale cost of those jars of sauce, it could lower the retail price, too, and still make money. In fact, by lowering the selling price, Walmart could go back to its first way of making money. When the price goes down, customers may be tempted to buy two bottles of pasta sauce at a time instead of one—so Walmart sells more sauce.

Of course, the pasta sauce factories eventually insisted they could not squeeze out any more savings to pass on to Walmart. At which point Walmart realized it needed to take a look at how that sauce got made. Perhaps if Walmart told its customers that it had decided to go green, it could sell more bottles of pasta sauce. So Walmart executives came to believe that they had to reshape their marketing strategies along the lines of a Malthusian world view, a view that emphasized sensitivity to ever increasing scarcity. Walmart would have to become sustainable.

In the summer of 2009, Walmart invited a thousand suppliers, business associates, and sustainability experts to a "milestone meeting." At this meeting, the company announced plans to eliminate twenty-two million tons of greenhouse gas emissions from its products. The company also introduced the idea of a sustainability index.

"I like metrics," Walmart CEO Mike Duke declared. "If you can't measure it, you can't manage it." And no doubt, Walmart possessed the capability of crunching as much sustainability data as might come its way. Not only is Walmart the world's largest corporation, it owns the country's second most powerful computer, after the Pentagon.

It was inevitable that as Walmart sought the metrics of a sustainable future, its interests would intersect with the consortium of growers, food processors, academics, and environmentalists known as the Stewardship Index for Specialty Crops. The measurements and formulas that had begun to emerge from the Stewardship Index's efforts, particularly the relative weightings of the water, nitrogen, and pesticides required for conventional agricultural production, were right in line with the efforts of the Walmart executives charged with calculating the life-cycle inputs and emissions of all of their food.

The Stewardship Index had collected a lot of information, and Walmart wanted it. Perhaps Walmart could scoop up all of the agricultural data collected by the Stewardship Index and feed the numbers into its own computer. Then it could decide on its own sustainability number, level, or code for each food product on its shelves. In fact, Walmart's sustainability numbers were destined for product labels so that consumers could grasp the essence of Walmart's environmental consciousness without having to bother with all of the intricate formulations.

The precise design of Walmart's sustainability label has been shrouded in secrecy, and many of the men and women I met on the tomato sauce trail expected that all of their measurements would be printed in small type on something that resembled an ingredients list: an account of all the water and diesel and energy and pesticide used for every product, along with every deleterious emission spewed into the sky, sunk into the soil, and spilled into stream and sea. But one source suggested that Walmart's sustainability label would not look anything like an ingredients list; it would instead take the form of a speedometer with a needle that swung from green to red to represent the degree to which a product was sustainable—or, at least, sustainable according to the definition of sustainability Walmart's sustainability department had defined for itself.

Walmart's sustainability labels would be the most ambitious environmental marketing concept ever deployed. And since the world's number one retailer was demanding an account of all of the inputs and outputs that lay behind its products, Walmart could be confident that every supplier up and down the food chain would do everything it could to meet the new requirements for measuring the future of planet Earth.

Above all, Walmart's sustainability strategy was about sales, and all of its measuring and managing was just another way of demanding that its suppliers sell their products cheaper. Despite Walmart's goal of eliminating greenhouse gas emissions, and despite the notion of a Walmart sustainability index, if any supplier had come back and said something like "We're making Wheaties greener, but it's going to cost you fifteen cents more a box," Walmart would most likely have responded, "Wrong answer."

Everyone understood the new marketing strategy. Goaded by Walmart, the efforts of transnational food retailers to deliver every last grain of life-cycle data would force massive efficiencies and reformations, which in turn might prove to be the best way to provide everybody on Earth with as much inexpensive, healthy, and delicious food as possible. Of course, considering two centuries of Malthusian disputes about the potentials and the limits of the world's resources, there would be those who disagreed with Walmart's methods. But given the global reach and power of Walmart, a number of sources who were otherwise eager to talk to me did not want their names (or too much of anything about themselves) connected to their quotes about Walmart.

One of my nonattributable sources had been involved in Walmart's sustainability projects and had also attended a series of high-level Stewardship Index meetings only to realize that no matter how many gigabytes of information Frank Muller and his brothers might collect from their tomato megafarm and no matter how many KPIs Unilever might collect from its tomato-smashing factories, the long-sought measurement, the sustainability unit, would remain elusive. "The data was absolute crap," my source said. The Stewardship Index meeting he attended was about canned pasta sauce, and all of the conversation had been about the can. "Assessment data sets are great for mining," he said, "but irrigating tomatoes in the Sacramento Valley and the amount of water used, that is a huge issue. To say it doesn't even register on the radar screen is just bullshit."

No one could argue that fresh water was not an essential resource, but how could the sustainability experts fit water into the same equation as the can and all of the effort and energy necessary to mine, melt, and mold that metal? Then again, how could anyone quantify every possible effect of the Ragú life cycle, from nitrogen use to pesticide spray to the label on the jar to the ink on the label to the air miles that brought that ink to that label and so on and so forth in endless backward reticulation? After years of data accumulation, after endless numerical analyses of frozen peas, packaged tea, and process tomatoes, the problem remained. No one knew how to measure a unit of sustainability.

Is it truly better for both humanity and planet Earth if everyone eats local tomatoes, or is it just as ecologically efficient to boil high-pulp hybrids, ship them, process them, bottle them, and ship them once again across the country and the world? We may never know.

As all of the raw data kept pouring in, the debate about measurement took a backseat to an even greater dispute.

Behind closed doors, the question that troubled most of the agribusiness sustainability indexers did not concern the relative merits or demerits that the sustainability metrics might possess, or the firewall between their data and the public, but the question of who would, at the end of the day, own all of the data. For everyone had come to realize that the data about the food were more valuable than the food itself. "Who will know everyone's measurements?" asked my source. "Who controls the data controls everything."

Despite its press releases and Web-streamed sustainability conferences, Walmart did not strike me as the food vendor most concerned with the scarcity of the planet's resources. What Walmart wanted was to retain its monopoly of market share, and, like Frank Muller and Unilever, Walmart used overall productivity as its measurement—which means money. Since Walmart was driving the effort to index sustainability, and the essence of sustainability was data, and all that data meant money, if anyone was going to get the money, it was going to be Walmart.

So I booked a ticket to Arkansas.

I ambled past the pine trees and the waterfalls that graced the entryway of the Applied Sustainability Center of the Sam M. Walton College of Business. The Applied Sustainability Center was one of the world's first sustainability think tanks, and since its inception it has received millions of dollars from Walmart. I had an appointment with the center's executive director, a professor of corporate measurement named Jonathan Johnson.

Johnson had assembled a team of cross-disciplinary researchers and technologists and handed them the task of constructing the most complicated measuring device ever conceived: a tool that could quantify the overall environmental impact of every retail product. Such a measuring tool could be deployed not only by Walmart but also by the likes of Domino's Pizza, Leprino Foods, Tyson Foods, Unilever, and every other major and minor food processor and producer in the world.

Johnson's group had been examining the widest variety of approaches, from ecological engineering and energy audits to uncertainty analyses, not to mention a recent study funded by the Applied Sustainability Center that analyzed other sustainability centers.

Professor Johnson is a thin man, with the sleepless eyes of an academic who knows there is much too much to know and not enough time to learn it. We sat in his book-lined office and discussed fresh water and the global tomato, herbicides, fertilizers, Thomas Malthus, Frank Muller, Big Pizza, and the current effort to account for every input and emission of everything we buy and sell. With us sat a young physicist who was, Johnson told me, an expert in Internet technology. This young man had been invited to the meeting to fill me in on any detail of sustainability number crunching that might escape the executive director.

In the middle of our conversation, Johnson noted that the Stewardship Index for Specialty Crops was not alone in its quest to define and quantify sustainability. "Sure," I said. "I know about Scientific Certification Systems, the American National Standards Institute, Greentick, and GreenBiz."

Johnson nodded slowly, then spoke as though this were the first day of an undergraduate survey course. "There are more than 350 sustainability certifications out in the world," he told me, and all of them compete with one another. "Products are already being graded, whether they like it or not," he said. "You've got greenwashing out the wazoo."

But no one knows how to define sustainability, I said. How can we have competing certifications when no one knows how to compare the can to the water to the diesel to the insecticide? At that point the expert in Internet technology made a profound observation. "Sustainability," he said, "is a clusterfuck."

The young physicist smiled. Dr. Johnson smiled. And as a favor to the Applied Sustainability Center, I copied the comment in the section of my notebook headed "Not for Attribution."

PART II

Looking for the Killer App(etizer)

Yet Nature is made better by no mean
But Nature makes that mean; so over that art
Which you say adds to Nature, is an art
That Nature makes. You see, sweet maid, we marry
A gentler scion to the wildest stock,
And make conceive a bark of baser kind
By bud of nobler race. This is an art
Which does mend Nature—change it rather; but
The art itself is Nature.

—William Shakespeare, *The Winter's Tale*

Whoever invents or discovers any new and useful
process, machine, manufacture, or composition of
matter, or any new and useful improvement thereof, may
obtain a patent therefor.

—U.S. Patent and Trademark Office, *Manual of
Patent Examining Procedure*

5

The Nucleotidal Wave

The effects of radium on plant cells were first noted in 1908, and by 1973 twenty-four crops had been released with improved disease resistance based on mutations that had occurred as a result of radiation. Today, more than half of the crops grown in the United States have been genetically transformed through either chemical-induced or radiation-induced mutation. This is not a widely known, much less widely contemplated, fact about our food.

Radiation- or chemical-induced genetic alteration is called *mutagenesis*, and the fruits and grains that have been transformed in this way may be grown conventionally, hydroponically, or however you choose to plant, fertilize, and weed your backyard garden. Many of these mutated varieties are grown organically and sold under the organic label. When I learned that certain foods had been created decades ago by mutagenic processes—foods that are now sold as organic—I realized I had no idea what a "genetically modified" crop really is. But I did understand that what we eat is not what it appears to be or what most people believe it is.

In fact, while all of the mutagenic varieties of fruits and vegetables are created through exposure to radioactivity or carcinogenic chemicals (even the varieties that are grown organically and sold as organic), none of these mutants, technically speaking, are what is now called genetically modified food. *Genetic modification*, it turns out, has its own extremely narrow definition, a definition that hinges on the history of chemistry. Not until late in the twentieth century did molecular biologists figure out how to manipulate the genetic material of food without cross-breeding, without mutating the cells with radiation, or without dousing them with carcinogens. Only these latest methods qualify as genetic modification.

It is often reported that biotech crops are the fastest adopted technology in the history of modern agriculture. On more than 370 million acres of global farmland, genetically modified agriculture is a done deal. Those in favor of genetically modified crops and livestock argue that laboratory innovations have helped to produce delicious, inexpensive, and healthy food for everybody. They argue that genetic modification produces better food than ever, high-yield and next-generation drought-resistant crops, flood-resistant crops, insect-resistant crops, herbicide-resistant crops, and crops that can be grown under harsher conditions than the older varieties, including less water, colder winters, hotter summers, saltier soils, and more carbon dioxide in the atmosphere. In other words, despite an increasingly nasty and brutish environmental future, genetically modified crops will be there to answer the caloric requirements of human beings.

On the other hand, critics of genetic modification see the crops as a Pandora's box of genetic pollution. They see Charles Darwin's theory of adaptation and evolution exploited by big business and turned into molecular moneygrubbing and a sure path to food failure. Bill Freese, a science policy analyst at the Center for Food Safety, told me that out of fifty thousand gene transfer attempts, only four traits had made it to the market. "There have been over 150 organisms, and over something like sixteen hundred different genes involved in these field trials," he said. "And these are the ones that are not confidential. There's a lot of secrecy here."

I imagined hydroponic caches of bizarre fruits and vegetables developing behind the locked doors of clandestine laboratories. "Have you ever thought why these transgenic experiments are called 'events'?" continued Freese. "What is an 'event'? It's not repeatable. If you do a well-controlled experiment, you should be able to repeat it. But what they're doing is taking the fruits of this and introducing it to the food supply."

On the microscopic level, Freese told me, gene transfers may result in never-before-seen "fusion proteins," strange new food molecules, and all sorts of bioactive substances. The gene transfer techniques that define genetic modification induce DNA deletions, disruptions, rearrangements, scramblings, fragmentations, translocations, superfluities, and redundancies—any of which may instigate any number of invisible and unforeseen traits and, conceivably, contaminations. Food genes could lose their function, not express themselves as before, or be silenced. "Sometimes these mutations in the crop genome will result in gross defects," said Freese. "There's a very high failure rate. A lot of the experiments just aren't viable. Scientists don't know what they're doing."

But when I spoke to the botanists, the molecular biologists, and the historians of science, I heard a different story. The genetic alteration of nature is a continuum, they explained. Every act of domestication, every act of pollination, and every act of cross-breeding had changed the genetic makeup of human food. Everything we eat and drink—from soup to nuts and espresso afterward—has been genetically altered from its original form. Transforming the code of the genome was simply the logical next step. In order to deliver enough food to feed the world, they said, we had to take that step. "The time when people decide to change is when they are under stress," said Ofer Bar-Yosef, a professor of anthropology at Harvard University who has spent a great deal of his career studying Neanderthals. "We are under stress right now," he continued, "so we are undergoing change." The Neanderthals, you may recall, disappeared from the face of the earth thirty thousand years ago.

Once upon a time, nymphs, sprites, and spirits ruled every cavern, tree, field, and brook, and a meal was plucked from a bush, scooped from the mud, or carved from the carcass of some unfortunate creature. Then everything changed. A tribe of infidels and heretics decided it could no longer leave something as important as breakfast, lunch, and dinner to the vagaries of chance and the whimsy of the gods. These revolutionaries drained lakes, rerouted rivers, chopped down forests, and slashed straight into the guts of Mother Earth. They were the first farmers.

Ten thousand years of meddling with food has not made the meddling any more popular, even if the history of civilization has hinged on the science of food. Assyrian bas-reliefs and Sumerian cuneiform tablets depict artificial pollination—and manipulating the sex life of plants was one of the first technological feats that enabled our world of abundant fruits and vegetables, meat, bread, and chocolate.

What set the earliest agriculturalists apart from the even earlier hunter-gatherers? As the first farmers denuded nature, hoarded seeds, and engineered crops, they most likely appeared to be mad scientists, coaxing mutant monsters from the black earth. Of course, we no longer think very much about the fact that almost everything we eat has been domesticated and that domestication implies a history of human intervention. In fact, most people are unaware that the typical supermarket and green market varieties of apples, oranges, lettuce, and raspberries are not at all the same as their wild cousins.

Domesticated fruits and vegetables are generally larger than their undomesticated counterparts. They are sweeter and more aromatic. Compared to their great-great-grandparents, modern fruits and vegetables have lost their fuzz, their fiber, their thorns, and their puberty. A modern tomato—heirloom, organic, process, vine-ripened, or otherwise—bears little resemblance to its puny, sour, undomesticated relations that sprout in the Peruvian Andes. Tomato breeding has changed tomatoes down to the DNA, and the successful varieties that have found their way into our supermarket carts have been cloned and cloned again.

The red jungle fowl of Thailand eventually became a Perdue chicken. The extinct aurochs of the Fertile Crescent eventually became Holstein cows. The primeval apples of

Kazakhstan eventually became Gala and Red Delicious. Ancient tillers of the earth needed at least three hundred years to domesticate corn and more than a thousand years to domesticate wheat. But no one really knows how weeds first became crops.

Did mongrel grains serendipitously meld together and sprout from the sewage dumps of sedentary fishing tribes (a current theory), or was the domestication of wheat grasses, pomegranates, and fig trees a willful act of genius? The most ancient of these technologies created new forms of life. And our fear of Frankenstein predates Mary Shelley's monster.

In *The Winter's Tale*, William Shakespeare laced Perdita's voice with anxiety and disgust as she condemned "Nature's bastards," new varieties of flowers created by Elizabethan methods of artificial pollination. Not to worry, argued Polixenes, for "Nature is made better by no mean / But Nature makes that mean; so over that art / Which you say adds to Nature, is an art / That Nature makes."

When we talk about the genetic alteration of plants and animals, we rehash the arguments of Perdita and Polixenes. Are molecular meddlings—from the man-made pig and the gene-whacked salmon to the genetically modified soy that hundreds of millions of us consume each day in cookies, crackers, candy bars, and sodas—are these transformations condoned by the tools nature itself has given us, or are they freaks and abominations? In producing as much food as possible for as many people as possible by creating superseeds that promise superharvests—seeds laced with DNA from other species of plants and animals—we may be redeeming the world. However, we may also be aiding and abetting the destruction of nature as we know it.

Biochemistry may be destiny. Once food DNA was discovered, perhaps it was only a matter of time before our daily bread would fall victim to our infatuation with technology. But now that we can take apart and put together the chemical puzzle blocks of food, we can't ignore the game. We can't bury molecular biology underground and move on. We have to figure out what to do with the technology. What we do with it matters.

There was another reason I was interested in the molecules. I wanted to get to the bottom of the food problem, but everywhere I looked I found evasion. On the molecular level, I figured, the spreadsheets, the real estate costs, the numerical indexes, and the profit margins could no longer overwhelm the search for inexpensive, healthy, and delicious food for everyone. On the molecular level, food could only be itself.

So I decided to consider the chemistry and soon discovered that chemistry has infiltrated food. Unimaginably immense markets for purified caffeine, citrus pellets, dextrose, cassein, and whey dominate the transnational trade, not to mention the ingredients label. Industry buzzwords no longer feature nouns like *fruit* and *vegetable*—how quaint and twentieth-century! Now all the talk is about phytoboosts, hydrolyzed proteins, peptides, probiotics, and polyphenols. There's money in custom-made fermentation substrates and the ever more precise fractionalizations of harvest and slaughter into enzymes and increasingly abstruse compounds and emulsions.

Was all this chemistry simply a matter of squeezing every dollar from a cow or a corncob, another inevitable if unsavory by-product of industrial sustainability? Or was chemistry the way to better, cheaper, healthier, and more delicious food? If so, has the long history of food technology reached its apex in the science of genetic modification?

The greatest U.S. food technologist was arguably Luther Burbank, who bred thirty thousand new varieties of plums before he came up with his pitless prune and destroyed who knows how many thousands of failed seedlings before unveiling his white blackberry and his spineless cactus. In 1893 Burbank published *New Creations in Fruits and Flowers*, and few doubted that the book would assure him a place in the scientific pantheon. Journalists dubbed him a "seer," Henry Ford and Thomas Edison came to visit, and Lionel Barrymore portrayed him in the 1947 radio play *The Man with Green Fingers*. Today, the effects of Burbank's breeding may be appreciated at McDonald's, where every french fry descends from a variety he invented in the 1870s.

It was largely because of Burbank's extraordinary achievements in food science that the Plant Patent Act of 1930 amended U.S. patent law to provide botanists with a set of financial motivations to create new plant varieties. (Burbank was posthumously awarded U.S. plant patent numbers twelve through sixteen.) All of a sudden, plant breeding promised more than a little fame and a lot of strange new foods. There was money in it.

The Plant Patent Act of 1930 pushed food science forward and helped power agribusiness into the second most gainful enterprise in the nation (after pharmaceuticals). Companies like Dow Chemical, Monsanto, and Syngenta take enormous profits from their food patent operations, but the emergence of a custom-designed corn seed cannot be blamed on the modern world's seed giants. Hybrid corn appeared more than a century ago on the U.S. retail market, and the result back then was the same as the result today: general outrage. The reason: hybrid seeds lose their potency after a single generation.

For ten thousand years of agricultural history, seeds had been free for those who cared to gather them, a gift that ensured next year's harvest. But the newfangled scientific corn seeds of the 1880s and 1890s had to be cross-pollinated, packaged, and purchased anew every year. What farmer in his or her right mind would buy new seeds every year? Seeds could be gathered from the ground. Seeds were free. Seeds *wanted* to be free. But then the stalks of corn from high-priced hybrid seeds began to take home banners, medals, and ribbons at state fairs, and farmers recognized that these new products were packed with new genetic information and that agricultural information was not free.

For a while, the farmers complained that the new scientific seeds should be put in contests all by themselves. But after a few harvests, no one cared how the seeds had been produced, and no one cared that they were barren. No one had ever seen such beautiful corn. No one had ever seen such extraordinary yields. No one had ever made so much money.

Soon U.S. universities were constructing their own agriculture and livestock laboratories, and institutes of higher learning joined the new molecular science of food. In the 1920s, a professor of biochemistry at the University of Wisconsin named Harry Steenbock exposed milk to ultraviolet radiation, which increased its level of vitamin D. Steenbock had figured out how to use radiation to alter the chemicals in food, and with three hundred dollars of his own money he patented his method—at which point one of the world's largest companies, Quaker Oats, offered Steenbock a million dollars for the rights to use his technology to fortify its breakfast cereals.

Steenbock had created food's first killer app. But instead of selling his patent to Quaker Oats, he formed a partnership with the University of Wisconsin called the Wisconsin Alumni Research Foundation (WARF), and the partnership licensed Steenbock's method to Quaker Oats, along with a number of other dairies and pharmaceutical companies. Steenbock and the University of Wisconsin had formed a technology transfer office, the model for the intellectual property factories now common on campuses throughout the world. Today, WARF has evolved into a patent-management agency worth more than a billion dollars.

In 1923, Steenbock understood that in order to guarantee cash flow from new food technology, food must be translated into a new language.

From his office in Taiwan, Dr. Thomas Lumpkin insisted that the U.S. government and U.S. citizens must stop taking food for granted. "There's a crisis right out in front of us," he said. "We have exploding economies in India and China that are going to suck up a lot of the resources around the world. They'll buy the food off the plate of America. We've got to get out there and reinvest in agriculture, and genetically modified organisms are part of the package."

Lumpkin, an expert in East Asian agriculture, is the director general of the World Vegetable Center, a nonprofit research institute devoted to increasing the production and consumption of safe vegetables for the poorest people in the world, those who live on less than a dollar a day. He explained that more than twenty-one million tons of eggplant are produced every year in the developing world, almost all of it in Asia, where aubergine is considered the king of vegetables.

He also told me that high levels of pesticides have been found in the drinking water of major cities in South Asia. These poisons were traced to areas directly adjacent to the cities where eggplant farmers had been spraying pesticides every morning and evening, delivering more than 140 pesticide applications before their eggplant harvests went to market.

In order to eliminate the toxic runoffs that have polluted urban water supplies, one of the World Vegetable Center's partner institutions—Lumpkin would not say which one—has been building a better eggplant, a special eggplant that has been altered by the addition of a gene that is toxic to the insects of southern India. "In genetic engineering, we take out the need to have this bacteria in a spray," said Lumpkin. "We've taken the gene for that insect toxin and put it in the plant."

No more pesticide spray, no more toxic runoff, no more polluted urban water supply. "There's just a tremendously desperate need for this whole science to be introduced at the lowest level and carried all the way through our public school system," said Lumpkin. "Society needs education to make the decision about this technology."

I told him I would try to understand.

• • •

In order to understand, I needed to see. So I went to Davis, California.

For fifty bucks an hour, the University of California–Davis Plant Transformation Laboratory, one of the premier genetic modification labs in the United States, will offer its services to anyone with a dish of DNA, a vegetable, and a mutation dream. It is where ordinary supermarket fruits and vegetables are converted into new and improved species, and it has been home to more than thirteen thousand "transgenic events," which is what molecular biologists call the results of blasting DNA from one life-form to another.

The man in charge of the Plant Transformation Laboratory is David Tricoli. Over the course of his career, he has worked with transgenic cantaloupe, transgenic squash, and transgenic zucchini, not to mention transgenic alfalfa, cherries, lettuce, rice, tobacco, and walnuts. He holds a number of patents for modifying cucumbers.

I gave Tricoli a call, he invited me out to take a look, and a few weeks later I found myself walking down the linoleum floor of Robbins Hall. I passed the green emergency shower and stopped in front of room 192, the Plant Transformation Laboratory. On the bulletin board someone had scrawled, in all capital letters, NOTHING IS REAL.

Noted.

It was warm inside Tricoli's laboratory and extraordinarily clean. Everywhere I looked I saw another budding baby plant, each shooting from a shallow layer of an antiseptic growth medium called agar, a gel that comes in pink, orange, blue, and black. Nowhere did I see a streak of mud or a speck of soil, and it occurred to me that within the heady, HEPA-filtered atmosphere of the Plant Transformation Laboratory, I was finally catching a glimpse of the foot soldiers who would fight and win the agricultural battles of the future. Either that, or this was the end of food as we know it. "A lot of what we do is plant stem-cell research," said Tricoli. "It's a powerful way to improve plants."

Thick ropes of electric cord snaked from the ceiling of the laboratory to three metal growth chambers, each ten feet tall. These double-doored high-tech greenhouses could have passed for walk-in freezers had it not been for the red biohazard stickers. Within these stainless-steel nurseries, thousands of newly developed plant breeds bathed beneath pink and blue fluorescent lights—childlike colors that matched their endless, artificial spring.

The tiniest transformants sprang from scores of round plastic petri dishes, each translucent root sucking up its own blend of multicolored nutrient. Tricoli pointed out his miniplots of transgenic peppers (green and hot), his transgenic potatoes (the world's fourth largest food source), and an impressive variety of transgenic lemons and limes.

I poked the touch-screen computer built into the door of one of the growth chambers, and the screen immediately morphed into a temperature graph. Perhaps if I changed some of the variables—relative humidity, leaf temperature, oxygen level—I might help the process along. But when I pressed the next button, the computer demanded my access code, at which point Tricoli explained that twenty-four hours a day, seven days a week, off-site technicians monitor the health and well-being of his transgenic plants. Within the growth chamber, new food is under constant surveillance. "Plants don't rest," said Tricoli. "They don't sleep. They're always growing. Here I think they have everything they need—all the sugar, all the carbon source, all the nutrients. They are pampered, that's for sure."

After the plants have matured inside the growth chambers, they will be wheeled across campus and repotted at the university's Controlled Environment Facility, where there are so many genetically transformed grains, vegetables, fruits, nuts, and tobacco plants that the humming aquamarine metal growth chambers take up an entire floor of an industrial warehouse-size building. Soon the new species will be strong enough to be double-wrapped and sent across the country to their owner-creators. And Tricoli will catch his last glimpse of the fruits and vegetables he midwifed into the world as his assistants prepare them for the rigors of FedEx.

David Tricoli's idol is Gregor Mendel, the Austrian monk who created the modern science of genetics. Like Mendel, Tricoli studied for the priesthood before he found biology, so I figured he might sympathize with the moral concerns, spiritual anxieties, and outright terror some people feel about the quiet stockpiling of a new generation of fruits and vegetables, all of them substantially different from the way they first appeared on Earth. Do people have any reason to fear food that seems on the surface to be completely natural but that beneath the skin is as programmed and manipulated as a Cheeto or a Twinkie? "I wouldn't understand why they would be afraid," said Tricoli. "But if people can pick it up, hold it, feel it, cook it, eat it, the fear goes away. In twenty, thirty years, I'm hoping it will be gone."

Tricoli told me he grew up in a household of six brothers and sisters. "We ate," he said, "but we didn't eat good. Spaghetti two, three times a week. Homemade tomato sauce. When I was a kid we always got the bagged apples because they were really cheap. I remember one Christmas, asking for those huge apples and oranges in my stocking."

He entered the field of genetic modification to give the world more food, better food, healthier food, food that would not need so many pesticides and fungicides and herbicides, food that would not need so much water to grow, food that would not die in flood or drought or extremes of heat and cold. "People don't realize that three hundred years ago, a lot of people didn't have enough food for the entire year," he said. "We have no concept of that. We've lost the concept of how precious food is. If we didn't have enough to eat and genetically modified foods were available, there would be no debate. We'd jump all over it."

Today there is enough food to feed the world. And by almost every estimate, the UC-Davis Plant Transformation Laboratory has been a model of success. Delegations from Nigeria, Indonesia, Thailand, Malaysia, Vietnam, Colombia, and Brazil have toured the premises. European visitors have come from Austria, Bulgaria, Croatia, Denmark, Estonia, Germany, Greece, and Spain. Not to mention China, which has sent both its minister of agriculture and its deputy chief officer of agricultural genetically modified organisms.

But despite the Plant Transformation Laboratory's international renown, despite the advances in plant stem-cell research, despite the twenty-four-hour off-site ultrasecure surveillance of the growth chambers, despite thirteen thousand transgenic events, and despite Tricoli's hopes and dreams, transgenic fruits and vegetables still seemed less like food and more like a data stream or software, the source code for a program yet to be written or sold.

The genome of an eggplant possesses more than a thousand megabytes of data, roughly equivalent to the information embedded in 250 MP3 files. But when it comes to holding information, an eggplant is much more efficient than an iPod, for each microscopic plant cell holds all of the thousand-plus megabytes. I had thought that investigating food molecules would lead to something small, but here was something huge. Here were the new frontiers of science and ownership, for it was becoming increasingly clear that whoever staked a claim to all that data could earn a lot of money from it.

So once again the data started a fight. The environmental movement, the organic food movement, the locavore movement, the slow-food movement, the edible movement, the good-food movement, and the world peasant movement have vowed to resist genetically modified crops. Meanwhile, the molecular biologists sneer that all of these assorted activists are ill-informed, reactionary, self-centered, and elitist. The desire to produce inexpensive, healthy, and delicious food for everyone has turned into a big argument.

I needed to know more about the relationship of the molecules and the money, so I booked a trip to one of Ohio State University's experimental research stations, where I met a woman named Esther van der Knaap, who may have more to do with the future of tomatoes than anyone I met at Domino's, Unilever, or Frank Muller's megafarm.

Van der Knaap is a plant geneticist who has toiled for years on a problem that never would have occurred to me: the isolation and analysis of the genes that program the shape of a tomato. Her goal is neither to save tomato farmers from tomato viruses nor to create a better-tasting or a more nutritious tomato. Instead, she wants to engineer a square tomato—the kind of tomato that Heinz or Unilever might prefer to the round variety, particularly when it comes to packing as many as possible into square cardboard boxes. Along the way, van der Knaap is also trying to unlock the secret of a long, cucumberlike tomato shape, the kind of tomato Burger King, McDonald's, or Wendy's might desire so they could get more perfectly round, hamburger bun–size slices out of each individual fruit. Once van der Knaap has discovered the genetic sequences of squares and tubes, she will be well on her way to her goal: a comprehensive, genomic Fruit-Shape Index.

I found van der Knaap in her laboratory, staring into a computer screen that was running a proprietary program called Tomato Analyzer. I stared, too, at tomato coordinates. I had seen industrialized fast food bereft of most of the qualities that make food seem like food. I had seen food turned into a series of spreadsheets and equations. At last I was face-to-face with truly virtual food.

Over the past several years, van der Knaap told me, she and her colleagues had used Tomato Analyzer to help them isolate two fruit-shape genes. The protein they named OVATE controls the elongation and constriction that creates a shape that resembles a pear, and the protein they named SUN may constitute the genetic blueprint for all long fruit. Neither seemed to have much of anything to do with providing meals for anyone.

After an hour or so of our going over her scanning programs and shape algorithms, Professor van der Knaap led me
downstairs to her hothouse, a glass building that rumbled and
buzzed and hissed. Huge fans and industrial lights towered
above concrete floors spiderwebbed with plastic irrigation
lines. Here were thousands upon thousands of tomato plants,
not to mention wall-mounted pH monitors, digital weather
hazard alerts, an emergency shower and eyewash station,
and a tremendous steel door reinforced by twenty steel bars.
The steel door had been left open, revealing the inside of
an iron vault that could have passed for a medieval torture
chamber had it not been plastered with bright red biohazard
warning signs. "This is an autoclave," said van der Knaap. In
other words, this was her garbage disposal. No local dump
will accept chromosome-addled transgenic tomatoes, and
it is against the law to give experimentally altered feed to a
farm animal. So molecular biologists must take drastic measures: stamp them out, boil them to oblivion, and vaporize the
mutant stems and leaves back to primal muck. Thus the need
for a steel-girded fruit incinerator, the autoclave.

I reminded van der Knaap that she had promised to show
me her most recent batch of custom-shaped tomatoes, so we
strolled along a path of yellow hose, rusty pipe, and groan-
ing heating, ventilating, and air-conditioning equipment; past
walls tattooed with wires, dials, and switches, across floors
littered with industrial cleaning agents, chemical pesticides,
and motorized pot scrubbers.

As we walked down row after row of the molecular tomato
farm, van der Knaap explained that transnational fruit and
vegetable giants like Dole and Del Monte would not only

delight in the prospect of square tomatoes but might also appreciate square grapefruit and pineapples—the better to sit on conveyor belts. Perhaps, with the sale of cute little custom-shaped veggies just for kids—stars, hexagons, and trapezoids—Dole and Del Monte could increase their combined revenues far beyond their present eleven-figure level. Perhaps a whole new generation of sculpted lettuce and spinach could wash away the memory of the E. coli outbreaks. Small-scale farmers and grocers could benefit, too. "Shape really helps to sell a new product and create a niche market," said van der Knaap.

As we discussed numerous possibilities, we passed a chamber of tobacco plants, the leaves of which had been injected with tomato proteins. I wanted a closer look at these transgenic specimens, but van der Knaap would not let me enter that greenhouse. At experimental research stations such as this, fear of contamination runs high, for the slightest virus could send every infected stamen and sepal straight into the autoclave and stall shape-gene research for yet another year.

But van der Knaap made an exception for room 123, where she kept her latest crop of custom-shaped tomatoes. She pulled open the sliding door and there, among rusted snarls of ancient heating elements and piles of discarded watering cans, sat ninety-six spindly vines. There were no square tomatoes. There were no cucumber-shaped tomatoes. There were no hexagons or trapezoids. There were just those twisted shoots, some limp leaves, and a grow lamp.

I asked what kind of DNA she and Ohio State were trying to isolate in room 123.

"It's a shape gene," said the professor.

"What shape?" I asked.

She looked at me and smiled. "I'm not going to tell you."

But she did tell me that as soon as her genetics team could isolate tomato-shape DNA, Ohio State and van der Knaap would patent the genomic recipes for hearts, curlicues, and every other form and figure that one day might earn dividends. "I would get some money," said van der Knaap. "I'm the inventor."

6

The Code

Not too far from David Tricoli's Plant Transformation Laboratory is a small room sometimes referred to as the Chamber of Death. Here a professor of plant genomics named Pamela Ronald keeps her supply of *Xanthomonas*, a bacteria that could wipe out a great deal of the world's food supply.

Rice is one of the most inexpensive, healthy, and delicious ways to feed everyone on Earth. It nourishes more people than any other food. But the kind of bacteria kept in the Chamber of Death has devastated rice crops in China, India, Indonesia, Japan, Malaysia, the Philippines, Thailand, and Vietnam.

Japanese scientists were the first to try to kill the killer. They began research in 1901 but met with no success, and eventually the white lesions, leaf wilt, and total crop collapse typical of a *Xanthomonas* infection made its way beyond Asia. In the 1970s, the bacteria assaulted rice in Africa, the Americas, and Australia, and biologists began to fear a global epidemic. None of the usual paths to inoculation worked against this disease, so nearly a century after biologists had started their investigations, Pamela Ronald began to contemplate a new way to make rice immune to *Xanthomonas*.

The solution she considered was genetic modification. She knew that if she could solve the *Xanthomonas* problem, the world would be a better place. She knew that her solution—that is, if she could discover a solution—would constitute one of the greatest triumphs of food science in all of human history. It was hard for anyone to imagine a negative that could outweigh the positives. A better argument for a genetically modified food could not exist.

After showing my identification to the lab supervisor, signing in, and suiting up in one of those all-white lab getups, I walked into a room plastered with the now familiar red and orange biohazard stickers of genetic modification laboratories. I saw a few microscopes, a centrifuge, an incubator, and a freezer. The dead bolt on that freezer caught my attention. My guide, a staff researcher, put on a pair of rubber gloves, opened the glass-topped incubator, and brought out a petri dish of yellowish goo, which he pulled away from my outstretched hands. "I can't let you touch it," he said. The causal agent of the bacterial blight that threatens the crop that feeds half the world looked like a wad of old chewing gum.

Pamela Ronald has spent her professional career trying to protect rice. That was why, many years ago, when she was still a graduate student, she put in a request to the

International Rice Research Institute in the Philippines for a sample of a hybrid descended from a rare variety known as *Oryza longistaminata*, a wild rice species that had long been gathered by the Bela tribe of Mali. *O. longistaminata* tastes lousy and offers unexciting yields, but this particular variety of rice had one thing going for it: it was virtually immune to the lesions of the Asian rice blight *Xanthomonas*.

Ronald and her colleagues at Cornell University—and then at the University of California–Davis—spent half a decade tracking down the precise location of *Xanthomonas* resistance within the genome of the hybrid rice sample from Mali. The professor knew that if she could isolate the disease-resistant gene from among the hundreds of millions of DNA pairs that defined *O. longistaminata*, her team could eventually insert that particular protein sequence into any variety of rice they wished, from long grained to sticky, sushi, or Uncle Ben's. This was just what her team accomplished in 1995, when it introduced a *Xanthomonas*-fighting gene into a once widely cultivated glutinous rice variety called Taipei 309 and created an immunity to disease where none had been before, a genetically modified immunity that could be passed from one generation to the next.

Ronald had inoculated rice. Her chemistry had insured the world's supply of inexpensive, healthy, and delicious food. The plants she had created were growing here, at UC-Davis, and I had to see them.

DNA was the purest form of food I had come across. It was unvarnished information, the ultimate market-delivered component. It was invisible, it was intellectual, it was scientific, and best of all, it was property. It made the wonders of global pizza look crude and primitive. It made sustainability seem beside the point.

For DNA is more than food. All of those millions of sequences meant that the glorious diversity of creation could be counted and accounted, then mixed and matched. So while the system might appear broken to those who made food from seeds, soil, and water, to those who hold patents the system was doing just fine.

It is a distinct possibility that one day, in the not too distant future, all of the genetic material in the world will be someone's property, owned and managed by corporations, governments, and very rich people. I realized this likelihood early one morning in Corvallis, Oregon, as fog engulfed the Willamette Valley and I pulled up to a battered sign:

UNITED STATES DEPARTMENT OF AGRICULTURE
AGRICULTURE RESEARCH CENTER
WORLD PLANT COLLECTIONS
"CONSERVING DIVERSITY FOR THE FUTURE"

Razor wire sparkled atop the chain-link fence, but the gate to the federal government's parking lot had been left open and unattended. I coasted past the guardhouse, the surveillance cameras, and the American flag.

When I entered the low-slung building at the end of the pitted parking lot, I found myself face-to-face with a floor-to-ceiling map of the world. I settled into a government-issue molded plastic chair, gazed at the map, and waited to meet the fruit prospector.

A fruit prospector travels the world in search of new fruit, and if and when she finds what she is looking for, she brings it back to the United States—along with a portfolio of the fruit's associated intellectual property rights. I was under the impression that we had already discovered all the fruit that was out there, but Kim Hummer, the research leader in Corvallis, set me straight. She sat behind a large desk in a corner office dominated by glass-front cabinets that held a staggering variety of hazelnuts, which happen to be her particular specialty. I thought a filbert was a filbert, but as it turns out, the standard supermarket hazelnut is a global all-star plucked from an extraordinary roster of round and oval nuts that come in all shades of tan and brown.

Hazelnuts were not going to feed anywhere near as many people as Domino's and Pizza Hut. About half of the people on the planet don't even know hazelnuts exist. The flavoring for praline may not have much to do with delivering delicious, healthy, and inexpensive food to the masses, but the nature and history of how hazelnut genes became U.S. government property might provide perspective.

Hummer led me out of her office to the world map in the lobby and began to outline her recent travels along the Pacific Rim in search of berries, fruits, and nuts. She traced her finger from Oregon up to Washington, then on to Alaska and across the Bering Strait to the Northern Pacific islands of Ostro Iturup, which are nothing much more than a dozen underwater volcanoes that once spewed a great deal of lava into the Sea of Khotsk. Hummer moved down through Siberia and finally settled on the Sakhalin Islands, where archaeological excavations indicate that human beings had been foraging for food since the Neolithic Stone Age. "Sakhalin has been taken over by oil interests," said Hummer, "but there happen to be some strawberry populations there, too."

The goal of fruit prospecting has always been diversity. An alpine fruit or a desert berry might supply vitamins and minerals when other fruits and berries fail and provide insurance in cases of drought and flood, heat waves and cold snaps. Given the right heredity, the right hybridizing, and the right technology, stockpiles of such plants might not only deliver better food to larger populations but also bolster national security.

Writing does not exist before agriculture. There are no records of the first search for food, so the formal history of fruit conquest begins only about three thousand years ago, when Egypt's first and only female pharaoh, Hatshepsut, sent explorers to the northeastern coast of Africa in search of pomes, a fruit family that includes loquats, medlars, pears, quinces, and, most famously, apples. Ever since the victories of Hatshepsut, new foods and new countries have been exploited together. When Christopher Columbus discovered America, he returned with maize. When Sir Joseph Banks sailed around the world with Captain James Cook, he brought back thirteen hundred plant species the Old World had never seen. Hernán Cortés returned with his *xtomatl* seeds.

And so the search for food has always possessed its politics. Before there was an arms race, the Russians and the Americans engaged in a fruit race. David Fairchild, perhaps the greatest of all American fruit prospectors, discovered more than two hundred thousand new plants, including scores of dates, mangoes, nectarines, and pistachios. His Russian counterpart, Nikolay Vavilov, traveled five continents in search of cereal.

In 1993, the Convention on Biological Diversity declared genetic resources to be the property of the country in which they reside. In other words, every country owns the genetic codes of all the DNA that might be discovered within its borders. Before anyone can go out into the world to claim ownership of any food that he or she may find, that food's legal status must be negotiated and bilateral agreements signed. "We cannot collect in China," said Hummer. "They want all the rights." As does Chile. Which is how the discovery of new food has come to depend on lawyers.

I left the Chamber of Death and set off down the hall to a large, light-filled room that did, after a fashion, resemble what one might expect from Dr. Frankenstein's laboratory. An exotic variety of centrifuges, vortex mixers, spinners, shakers, and voltage boosters rumbled and sputtered and whirred as more than a dozen syringe-wielding scientists bent over beakers and test tubes of yellow, blue, and clear liquid. There was a great deal of brown liquid on the premises, too, most of it labeled HAZARDOUS WASTE. One lab technician worked next to a small white box labeled TRANSFORMANTS and gazed at a histogram that had an arresting, single-word title: MUTANT. The shelves were piled with boxes and boxes of seeds.

One room off to the side of the laboratory housed the stainless-steel computer-controlled greenhouses within which scores of rice plantlets were flourishing beneath fluorescent lights. They all looked healthy, even if each had been syringed full of the *Xanthomonas* virus. Their new DNA had made them immune. Next to the rice plants sat dozens of altered tobacco plants and a few varieties of switchgrass that had been genetically transformed for experimentation in cellulosic bio-fuel technology.

I could have poked around that laboratory all day, but Pamela Ronald wanted to talk in her office, where Indian art adorned the walls. One batik caught my attention: three women up to their knees in the mud of a rice paddy. For five thousand years India's harvests had flourished or been devastated by disease—as deemed by luck or nature. But luck and nature were no longer the only players in the game. Ronald explained that she had recently begun to collaborate with a computational scientist at the University of Texas in Austin who had predicted that more than two thousand genes will eventually be understood to control rice's response to disease. "It is too much for the human brain," said Ronald. "This is a new time in science, and you cannot establish that an entire field cannot be useful."

Why, she wondered, do those who believe in evolution, climate change, and stem-cell research stop believing in modern science the moment it comes to what thay eat? Why, when there is so much complexity, importance, and nuance to the issue of our food, do new breeding techniques elicit a simplistic response from otherwise deep-thinking people? "Children are dying," said Ronald. "It's a mistake to shut out any technology. In the United States we have iodized salt, iron supplements, vitamin D–enriched milk and orange juice, and lots and lots of vitamins. We take it for granted. You can't let people die of malnutrition because you don't like the *concept* of the tool that can save them."

"There are one billion people in the world living like us," she continued. "One billion are starving, and 80 percent of the bottom billion are subsistence farmers. How do you bring these people up? Farming techniques, seeds, fertilizer . . . " Her voice trailed off. "I'll give a talk, and 90 percent of it will be about water and land degradation in Bangladesh. But the question people have is 'I hear genetically modified crops will be a problem for my child.' The larger issues are still not at the forefront."

I glanced at Ronald's office bookshelves, which featured the expected academic fare—*Plant Pathology* and *Lecture Notes on Genetics*—along with a few more compelling titles: *Pandora's Picnic Basket*, *The Frankenfood Myth*, and, rather blatantly, *Risk*. Open on her desk lay a book called *Banana*— which seemed like a good opportunity to change the subject.

Bananas are one of the world's most important foods, she told me, a dietary staple for a hundred million people. But a bacterial disease was now advancing through eastern Africa, threatening to destroy crops and spark food inflation and malnutrition. "The bacteria is spreading," said Ronald, who had already begun to work with molecular biologists in Nairobi, Kenya. "We are thinking about a genetically modi-fied banana."

As I made no comment, she turned to her computer, which flashed with an image of the weed *Arabidopsis*, the first plant genome ever to be sequenced. The full *Arabidopsis* genome possesses something on the order of a million base pairs, and Ronald explained that the gene sequencing project had taken seven years, employed five hundred people, and cost seventy million dollars. "In 2011 that same project would take two to three minutes and cost ninety-nine dollars," she said. "Now we have collected many rice genomes, and we can really mine the genetics for drought tolerance, heat tolerance, flood tolerance, resistance to bacteria, and nourishment. Everything we care about is embedded in these plant genomes."

Pamela Ronald's disease-resistant, genetically modified, potentially world-saving rice grows to maturity down the block from her laboratory, just off Health Services Drive in greenhouse 715, a tremendous glass-roofed, glass-walled hangar that can hold up to a hundred thousand rice plants. It was one hundred degrees outside that afternoon as the squirrels sprinted across the melting blacktop, but within greenhouse 715 the temperature held steady at a comfortable eighty-five degrees, with 30 to 40 percent humidity.

Off to one side lay plastic garbage bags of old rice experiments. The molecular janitors around here would soon cart the genetic waste off the premises to the UC-Davis autoclave, the great pressurized iron tank that would pulverize the altered genes back to elemental carbon and nitrogen and so halt the risk of any genetically ambiguous material floating down the road, through the scorching air, across the fields of central California, and up the nostrils of horses and cows.

Up and down the corridors of Ronald's greenhouse, transgenic rice grows alongside wild and domesticated varieties, so each vat of tall green marsh grass possesses its own coded label. Gene-shifted or not, all of the flat shoots had rough skin and pointy tips and were top-heavy with green kernels. The thick bunches of stalks shot up from black plastic paddies packed with mud and flooded with brown water. Most of the plants were a couple of weeks away from maturity, but others were six-inch babies, and others were dead. Much of the rice was Kitaake, a fast-growing, cold-tolerant variety. Other plants were Liao Geng. But most of them were Taipei. I stopped before a particularly tall, robust group of grasses. The code was Xa21-106/TP309.

Ronald explained that she and her team had created Xa21-106/TP309 through biolistic bombardment, a method criticized by many, including the food activist Michael Pollan. I asked Ronald about biolistics, in particular the level of risk associated with producing unintended consequences in the genomes of edible plants. "The risk of unintended consequences is: the plant doesn't grow," she said. "Well, who cares? Michael Pollan is not wrong about bombardment. You don't know where the gene is going. But does it matter? Pollan isn't wrong. He's just not asking the right questions."

If there was a hint of arrogance in her voice, perhaps it was because she had cracked the code. She possessed the killer app and had called it Xa-21. The tall grass I now stood before, the plant called Xa21-106/TP309, was the first disease-resistant transgenic rice that Ronald's team had created.

Just as the transnational agribusiness giants would have done with such a discovery, Ronald and UC-Davis filed the Xa21 gene with the U.S. Patent and Trademark Office and so ensured that the genetic sequence of *Xanthomonas* immunity would become their intellectual property. Soon after that filing, agribusiness giants Monsanto and Pioneer negotiated an option to license Xa21, and it looked as though Ronald's genetically modified grains would enter the global market.

But as the UC-Davis Office of Technology Transfer haggled over the terms for returning the inoculated rice genes to the International Rice Research Institute, Monsanto and Pioneer lost interest in the deal, and the commercial development of the technology stalled. Disease resistance, it turned out, did not have the same appeal for multinational food producers as it did for Ronald and UC-Davis, perhaps because Monsanto and Pioneer were already enjoying windfall profits from more lucrative agritech innovations, such as their Roundup Ready crops.

Pamela Ronald may want to save the world, but her killer app has never left the greenhouse. Even though the *Xanthomonas* bacteria remains a threat to Asian rice supplies, *Xanthomonas*-resistant rice is not grown anywhere on Earth aside from the sterilized plots of locked laboratories. Ronald has maintained a batch of Xa21-106/TP309 behind closed doors for more than a decade, but her rice is not much more than an academic curiosity. If molecular food can't earn rent, the molecules wither on the vine.

I have met many molecular biologists, and all were well-intentioned. They believed that in some way their work would unlock the truths of nature and help feed the world, and they moved forward as molecular biologists tend to do: single-mindedly—focused on the statistical probabilities of hybridization, the serendipities of mutation, and the bureaucracy of the U.S. Department of Agriculture. All of them were seeking the killer app. As a result, they were easy marks.

The global food game has become a property and an information game, and along the way the scientists, like the farmers, have been taken for a ride. After ten millennia of creating ever more precise agricultural tools, the scientists became the tools. And their much vaunted, much reviled molecules became the tools of the tools.

After I had spent weeks in laboratories and hours studying plant patent laws, these were my thoughts: Our age has fallen in love with the hyper, the meta, the virtual, and the derivative. But food is not virtual. And when we discuss food as though it were a patent right, a spreadsheet, an index, or a percentage of market share, we are no longer talking about food. As a result, more people than ever were going hungry.

PART III

Looking for a Leader

Food for all is a necessity. Food should not be a merchandise, to be bought and sold as jewels are bought and sold by those who have the money to buy. Food is a human necessity, like water and air, it should be available.

—Pearl S. Buck

7

Circus Maximus

Perhaps there really was a Golden Age of Plenty: a time and a place removed from everything we know of the world; an epoch without money, legal codes, or patented soybeans; a time without hunger. Such were the ever fruitful Arthurian plains of Avalon and biblical Garden of Eden, the Big Rock Candy Mountain of song, and the medieval mythical land of Cockaigne, where fish and fowl begged to be eaten and the rivers flowed with wine.

What seems to be progress is not always so. This point was driven home at the dawn of the Space Age, when famine was rampant, and many anthropologists who studied preindustrial societies began to argue that instead of slogging through a short, brutish life of Paleolithic poverty, so-called savage hunter-gatherers ate better than we eat, worked less than we work, slept a lot more than we sleep, and spent a great deal of their time hanging out, doing nothing. "The amount of hunger," Marshall Sahlins wrote in *Stone Age Economics*, "increases relatively and absolutely with the evolution of culture." Indigent or not, peckish primitives found ready supplies of mollusks, moths, and caterpillars. "Hunters," concluded Sahlins, "keep banker's hours."

This too was a myth. Even the most bucolic of the loin-clothed set don't particularly like to share, particularly around dinnertime. "Broil your rat with its fur on," goes the Maori proverb, "lest you be disturbed by someone." And Bemba tribespeople have a special name for the person who sits in your house and says, "I expect you are going to cook soon. What a fine lot of meat you have today!" That person is called a witch.

Eventually, as Stone Age economies progressed toward cash economies, warlocks and devils became poor people, which may have been a step in the right direction. Fifty years ago, when the Ford Foundation and the Rockefeller Foundation joined forces with the United Nations, the World Bank, and other organizations to end hunger, they concluded that the answer to not enough food was more food. And more food meant more of the food that the people who were already eating the most were eating the most of: corn, rice, soy, and wheat.

Hybrid seeds, along with the expanded use of fertilizers, herbicides, irrigation systems, and chemical pesticides, more than doubled cereal production in Asia over the next quarter century. Global harvests skyrocketed, the developing world found itself goggling at warehouses of grains, and the heady mixture of money, technology, and politics came to be known as the Green Revolution. The scientist behind the operation, Norman Borlaug, earned a Nobel Prize.

The successes of the Green Revolution indicated to almost everyone that the principles of agricultural science, international finance, and international trade could be successfully applied to the oldest and simplest problem of all: making sure everyone has enough food. But just two decades after the hunger experts launched the effort, they were blindsided by an astonishing reversal: the real number of hungry men, women, and children in the developing world began to climb again, from just over eight hundred million in the early 1990s to more than nine hundred million in the first decade of the twenty-first century.

Belatedly, the bureaucrats realized that Green Revolution policies had favored large landholders over small landholders, prosperous peasants over penniless peasants, and all that money, science, sophistication, and goodwill had actually *increased* economic inequality. The food bills of poor countries soared fivefold and sixfold, and since 2003 the overall proportion of hungry people on Earth has also been on the rise.

In the aftermath of the Green Revolution, the experts had to provide new reasons for world hunger, and these were no longer all about the food.

I had spent two decades as a food journalist, and hunger was the one subject I had not wanted to touch. Friends warned that no one would be interested in the topic; that it wouldn't sell; that immersing myself in the statistics would depress me; that the theme would make me a radical.

But I had become convinced that the food story was the story of not enough food. And now I began to suspect that the reason there was not enough food for some people in some places was the same reason there was not enough food for everyone everywhere. The breakdown in the system was global. The story was bigger than I had imagined.

By the end of the first decade of the twenty-first century, the worldwide price of food had climbed 80 percent, and for the first time in human history more than a billion people on the planet were going hungry. Rising prices for corn, cooking oil, rice, soybeans, and wheat sparked riots in Bangladesh, Cameroon, Ivory Coast, Egypt, Ethiopia, Haiti, Indonesia, and nineteen other countries. Not to mention Milwaukee, where a food voucher line of nearly three thousand people descended into chaos. ("They just went crazy down there," said one witness. "Just totally crazy.") In 2010, food prices spiked again, higher than ever.

What was the effect of rising prices on local vendors of fresh, healthy, inexpensive, and delicious food? Twenty-six-year-old Tarek al-Tayyib Muhammad Bouazizi earned less than five dollars a day selling fresh vegetables from an old wheelbarrow on a dusty street in the underpopulated, land-locked Tunisian town of Sidi Bouzid. As the global price of food inputs inflated, Bouazizi's minimal profits dipped, his debts rose, and when the local cops confiscated his cart on December 17, 2010, the food seller believed he had nothing more to lose. So he walked over to the only police station in Sidi Bouzid, sat down in the middle of the street, doused himself with gasoline, and lit a match.

The protests that followed throughout Tunisia sparked rallies, marches, riots, and strikes along a five-thousand-mile stretch from the Atlantic Ocean to the Persian Gulf: from Mauritania, Morocco, and Algeria through Libya, Egypt, and Sudan and all the way to Syria, Jordan, Saudi Arabia, Bahrain, Oman, and Yemen. As food prices took off, revolutions smoldered. For even as the price of global wheat rose and kept on rising, countries could not stop importing grain.

The largest grain importer of all is Egypt, whose people have possessed a taste for wheat bread and wheat beer ever since ancient farmers sowed seeds in the black soil left behind by the Nile's annual inundation. The wheat of ancient Egypt became the currency of ancient Egypt, the power behind the credit of the nation's central bank, the marrow of its financial system. And thousands of years after the last Pharoah, grain still ruled. When the price of wheat spiked in 2011, hunger, violence, and political turmoil descended like a biblical plague, and the result was revolution.

The United States was not insulated from the global food catastrophe this time, as it had been throughout the previous half-century. Forty-six million Americans now found themselves unable to put a full meal on the table. Across the country, the demand for food stamps reached an all-time high, and one in five American kids came to depend on food pantries. In Los Angeles, nearly a million people went hungry. Trader Joe's and Costco set limits on the amount of rice their customers could purchase. In Detroit, armed guards stood watch over grocery stores.

This time I did not ask why we can't have inexpensive, healthy, and delicious food available to everyone. This time I asked why a billion people were going hungry. I had no idea how closely related the two questions would be.

• • •

In 2008, at the height of the first global food crisis of the twenty-first century, I went to Rome. The U.N. Food and Agriculture Organization (FAO) had convened its once-every-five-year plenary meeting here, across the street from the Circus Maximus.

I watched the latter-day emperors arrive: presidents, prime ministers, plutocrats, puppets, dictators, and thugs left their limousines and paraded into the High-Level Conference on World Food Security and the Challenges of Climate Change and Bioenergy. That was quite a bit to consider in one conference, but as the number of starving people on Earth kept rising, hunger pushed aside all other concerns.

In 1996, the same group had met in the same chamber—112 heads of state and government representatives of the 186 member countries of the FAO—and at that time all had solemnly pledged to halve the number of hungry people in the world by 2015. Back then, almost everyone believed that globalized trade in agriculture would ensure universal access to food and nutrition. But this had not proved to be the case. The number of hungry people had not been halved. In fact, malnutrition and famine were increasing at a startling rate.

Three years after the 1996 meeting of the FAO, the United Nations approved its International Bill of Human Rights, which declared that every person has the right to be free from hunger. Then, in 2000, the United Nations adopted a set of eight Millennium Development Goals, the first of which was to end extreme poverty and hunger. But in the summer of 2008, the prices of wheat, corn, soy, and rice had doubled and doubled again, and food riots were erupting in more than thirty countries. The ranks of the hungry had spiked by 250 million, the most abysmal annual increase in all of human history. It was not an auspicious beginning for the millennium.

At the FAO conference in Rome, I sat through scores of hunger meetings and dozens of hunger press conferences and listened to one hunger speech after another. When the first day was done I ate pizza and drank red wine, then Italian beer, then sweet Italian lemon liqueur, and talked late into the night with hunger lobbyists from Bangladesh, Nigeria, and Poland, Oxfam, ActionAid, and the World Food Program. Eventually, a number of radical thoughts occurred to me, most of them unwelcome.

Perhaps, I thought, there was something wrong with the generally accepted wisdom that the developed nations of the Earth must help develop the undeveloped nations of the Earth. Perhaps development was a bad idea, particularly for the undeveloped. By trying to help, we were making things worse. Perhaps progress possessed a flaw—a nasty little tragic defect that somehow, some way, required hunger. For progress has not meant the end of hunger. In fact, it has meant quite the opposite.

Progress has been hunger's companion. The aftermath of World War I and the Russian Revolution saw hunger as the world had never seen. Between the world wars, hunger. The decade of World War II, more hunger. Fifty years ago, famine raged through China, and twenty million people died. It looked as though Thomas Malthus was right.

But Malthus was not right. For much of the twentieth century, global food production actually outpaced global population growth. And as the years have passed and the evidence has accumulated, it turns out that overpopulation may not be the cause of hunger after all. Malthus may have been correct to predict that as time went on, more people would starve to death. But he got the mechanism wrong.

Something other than the lack of food was keeping food from people's mouths.

A number of alternative hunger conferences had convened in Rome at the same time as the FAO's. Each opposed the high-level solutions that everyone knew would be proposed by the high-level politicians, solutions that would be debated and amended, and approved by the time the FAO High-Level Conference came to an end in a couple of days—at which point the question of world hunger could be put on the back burner for another five years.

The most attended and elaborate of these alt-hunger conferences was the Terra Preta Forum on the Food Crisis, Climate Change, Agrofuels, and Food Sovereignty, which was held in a punk rock venue that had once been a slaughterhouse. I showed up one evening and made my way through the rusted meat hooks that hung from the ceiling and cast shadows across the banners for the Asia Pacific Forum on Women, the World Forum on Fisher Peoples, and La Via Campesina's Russian constructivist rendition of farmers from four continents.

The international grassroots organizations' delegates to the Terra Preta Forum were not convinced that the money- and market-based metasolutions proposed by so many politicians and economists would put an end to world hunger. In fact, these men and women believed quite the opposite: that the structural adjustments and support provided to developing countries by the World Bank, the International Monetary Fund, and various donor governments of developed countries had actually thrown ancient agricultural practices into chaos, and the largest transnational corporate agribusinesses were the only ones who stood to gain. All in all, the solutions that nonhungry people foisted upon hungry people had ruined local livelihoods and wrought agricultural, ecological, and financial disaster across the face of the earth. Or, as one activist said: "Our global system is fucked."

Unlike the suit-and-tie crowd over at the FAO conference, the meat-hook assembly favored tie-dyed or green-tinted scarves emblazoned with images of wheat. There was a cohort of women in saris, South Americans in dusty cowboy boots, Englishmen in blue khakis and sensible walking shoes, and radical Italians in a variety of styles but easy to spot because of their excellent haircuts. I showed up after an early dinner and, fortified with two cappuccinos, entered the orbit of the antiglobalists.

A man named Michel Pimbert—the director of Sustainable Agriculture, Biodiversity, and Livelihoods of the International Institute for Environment and Development—called us to order. He was a slight man, pale and unsmiling, the activist's activist, devoted to the struggle. He closed his eyes and asked us to reimagine food.

I will admit that I snickered at the idea of sitting in a circle, holding hands, and imagining an end to the oldest problem on Earth. Then again, I have never been very good at imagining much of anything. But everyone else in the circle had closed their eyes, so I gave it a shot. I imagined everyone had enough to eat.

I imagined the hors d'oeuvres and the desserts, the fruits and the nuts, the grains and the vegetables, the birds and the fish. I thought of all the animals, but that made me think of Noah and his ark, which was a problem, because thinking about Noah made me think about Adam and how in the book of Genesis he had named all the animals. This in turn reminded me that Adam ate the forbidden fruit and as a result was cursed with tilling the soil by the sweat of his brow. And so my imaginary trip to the land of plenty ended up in the nasty, all too real world of subsistence farmers and hungry people.

I opened my eyes. Everyone else still had theirs closed, so I tried again, this time from a different angle. Since there actually was enough food to feed everyone on Earth, I imagined that I did not have to imagine all of the meals, because they already existed. So I began to consider what would happen if food were . . . *free*?

I tried to settle into this idea, but the allotted time for reimagining was up. Pimbert was speaking again, explaining that we could solve the world food crisis. The key, he said, was a new kind of spirituality. "Now that may sound wacky," he said.

It did, but at this point in the proceedings of the Terra Preta Forum, when we were asked to end the global food crisis by imagining the end of the global food crisis, nothing surprised me. "Indigenous people live by completely different cosmologies," Pimbert explained. "Knowledge is made. It's a social construction. We need to go beyond ecologically blind science. We need to decolonize economics." Any questions?

A woman in a sari asked Pimbert how she could implement organic methods on farms in Pakistan, where farmers did not want to farm organically—and would not get enough food from their land even if they did. "That's a good question," said Pimbert. So we tried to reimagine Pakistani farmers.

Of course, the antiglobalists were as right as anyone about a billion starving people—and more right than most. The whole thing had to be reimagined. Problem was, imagination was not a strong suit of the emperors.

On the first day of the FAO conference, Iran's president, Mahmoud Ahmadinejad, echoed the wisdom of the economist and sociologist Thorstein Veblen as he blamed world hunger on "conspicuous consumptions," which have "put all nations in the world on the verge of destruction." Such practices, declared Ahmadinejad, were satanic.

Mahmoud al-Habash, the Palestinian minister of agriculture, articulated a different perspective. "The main reason for the world food problem is political," he said. "The rich countries want to control the world." The way to end world hunger, explained Habash, was to end the occupation of the West Bank.

The pope sent an envoy with blessings from the Almighty and a few words of advice. "Feed the hungry," said his Eminence Cardinal Tarcisio Bertone.

I had begun to see a pattern: everyone was hiding behind something other than the problem. And the problem was not about getting food into mouths. That was a fairly simple project, as global hunger goes.

Getting food into mouths may have appeared to be the problem, but it was the problem upside down. Getting food into people's mouths was the final piece of the puzzle—the only thing left to do when everything else had been taken care of. Where the food came from, and how and why it came from where it did—those were the troubles. And those troubles were just as relevant for subsistence farmers in Guatemala as they were for rioters in Cairo and for nutrition-starved Americans afflicted by the fast-food, fake-food syndrome.

The rest of the day in Rome—and on into the evening— was taken up by cerebellum-melting recitations of crop yields, maniacal diatribes, plaintive excuses, unnecessarily complicated expositions that reiterated what everyone else had just said, and pathetic pleas for transnational mercy, all delivered by various heads of delegations. There were fifty statements per day, starting with the soon-to-be-deposed Hosni Mubarak and on through the heads of state of Japan, Brazil, Namibia, Vanuatu, Cuba, Croatia, Nevis, Tanzania, and Chad. The U.S. secretary of agriculture, Ed Schafer, was scheduled to address the assembly late in the afternoon. He would speak right after the Chinese agriculture minister, His Excellency Zhengcai Sun.

And so it went—a glut of information and accusation. Some delegates believed they understood what lay behind the crisis. Others knew they didn't—but gave their speech anyway. The emperors had come to Rome, and each would strut and fret five minutes on the stage. But even emperors can't solve world hunger by themselves. For that, they need the press.

The news stories that came from the conference varied in focus and emphasis but employed the same basic plot points. Biofuel production, caterpillar plagues, crop disease, diesel prices, drought, diminishing water tables, dwindling stockpiles, soil depletion, fear, flood, hoarding, war, and an increasing world appetite for meat and dairy had bubbled into a nasty market disequilibrium.

Luckily, for each of these problems there was a solution, and all of them had to do with money. But just because euros, dollars, riyals, and yuan had become intrinsic to everyone's hunger equation did not mean there was any lack of disagreement. While one faction of emperors advocated price-fixing and tariffs, another argued for free markets and the abolition of all tariffs. Decrease exports, demanded some; increase exports, pleaded others. Subsidize the rice trade; tax the rice trade. Purchase more grain from abroad; purchase less grain from abroad. Why hadn't I followed the money from the beginning?

Despite the abundance of suggested political and economic remedies, the general understanding at the FAO conference was that the old Green Revolution model of global hunger management no longer applied—even as the much older problem of not having enough to eat had accelerated. The age of shipping surplus rice and wheat across the oceans was over. Handing out candy bars and sacks of flour was not a long-term solution. Direct food assistance was dead. Now was the time for an entirely new conceptualization, which may have explained why rent support, social security, and subsidized electricity were now in the same conversation as irrigation and fertilizer.

The difficulty the world faced was no longer a logistical matter of shipping and handling the actual edible stuff but rather a matter once removed from food, a matter of money. Everyone could agree that when the price of your daily bread tops your daily salary, all the international food aid, sustainability numbers, and biochemical breakthroughs in the world will not make much of a difference.

And once it became clear that the food problem was not about the food, ironies popped up everywhere. Not until Rome did I begin to understand how many farmers could not afford to eat. When farmers can't make money farming, they lose the family farm—and they don't get jobs delivering pizza. When farmers can't make money farming, they simply can't make money, and that means they cannot buy the food they cannot grow.

At Walmart and Unilever and Domino's, I had witnessed all sorts of efforts to create as big a gap as possible between the price of the food coming off the farms and the price of the food in retail outlets and grocery stores. The gap did not exist because people in the supply chain are evil. The gap existed because people in the supply chain are smart. The less you pay for a tomato, the more you make on tomato sauce.

All of this indicated that the solution to world hunger was not to make a list of hungry people, then figure out how to feed them. Lack of money, not lack of food—that was the new answer to the old problem. But how much money? And what, precisely, should people do with it? And who should get how much?

The FAO's director general made it simple. Dressed in flowing blue robes, Jacques Diouf assured the greatest food assembly the world had ever seen that his organization could take care of the problem for thirty billion dollars a year. Then he requested donations.

After Diouf's speech, the president of Senegal articulated the problem even more succinctly. "This concept of assistance is now way out of date," declared Abdoulaye Wade. "Don't tell us what to do. We know what to do. You will see. We will change everything." Then Wade requested eight hundred million dollars for his own country's use, no questions asked.

"Modern agriculture requires capital and technology," noted Uganda's minister for water and the environment. "And for these inputs we need both local and foreign investors."

Nothing improved the human condition like cash—a fact that suggested new strategies not only for the global food crisis but for my own reporting.

You may be under the impression that wheat is one thing and corn another, but such is not the case. The more the politicians at the FAO conference pressed forward with the assumption that the problems of food could be solved with money, the more they warmed to the concept that food, like money, is interchangeable with any other global commodity. Food is not food as much as food is *value*.

A farmer may believe he has the most delicious cucumbers in the world, but the odds are that he would sell them to a man who planned to shoot them into space if he were willing to pay more than Walmart or Unilever pays. The dark earth from which that value emerges at the proper season each year is value, too. Arable land is just another placeholder in an ever expanding series of way stations for all of those euros, dollars, riyals, and yuan. As is water. As are nine thousand Domino's franchises worldwide. As were patented seeds.

There was one particular moment when the politicians at the FAO conference realized the new *food*, a moment when no one could avoid the conclusion that what we eat has less in common with the seasonal cycles of crops and more in common with the economic cycles of international commodities like gold and oil. This turn in the history of food came during the speech of Luiz Inacio Lula da Silva, then the president of Brazil. The subject was biofuels.

The political calculations that lie behind the global boom in turning the food business into the oil business have followed a fairly straightforward logic. Instead of depending on Middle East oil, countries should cultivate and harvest their own portion of the diesel fuel, car fuel, and jet fuel they require. This trend in sovereign agri-energy security had begun at the start of the millennium and accelerated in 2004. By 2010, two years after the FAO conference in Rome, 6 percent of all the world's barley, corn, millet, oats, milled rice, rye, sorghum, and wheat would never enter a living stomach—human, bovine, avian, or otherwise—but go straight to gas.

Today, just under half of the corn produced in the United States enters the so-called biofuel cycle. Grain brokers and traders in Chicago and New York—along with farmers, business owners, activists, food processors, and retailers up and down the food-supply chain—have laid the blame for recent spikes in hunger on the demand to produce biofuels.

Grains are not the only crop that once was food and now is fuel. Coconut oil, cottonseed oil, olive oil, palm oil, peanut oil, grapeseed oil, soybean oil, and sunflower seed oil have each been redirected from organic metabolisms to machines. Even cassava, the third largest source of carbohydrates in world meals, has become food for fuel.

And then there is the case of sugarcane. At the 2008 FAO conference in Rome, President Lula declared that Brazil, the largest economy in Latin America, was not using corn or peanut oil to make fuel. Instead, Brazil had spent a great deal of money, time, and effort figuring out how to extract ethanol from sugarcane. "In our country," said Lula, "over 40 percent of our energy comes from renewable sources. Biofuels are not the villain when cultivated responsibly."

The president told the assembly about the spectacular gains in fuel yields from the sugarcane grown in his country, sugarcane that had been genetically modified by killer apps created by Brazil's molecular biologists. As for the perception that Brazil's ever widening acreage of sugarcane plantation was invading the Amazon rain forest—well, said Lula, this was a senseless argument. He did not say a word about sugarcane's expansion into the Cerrado plateau, the richest and most biodiverse savannah in the world. Nor did he say a word about the rivers that have been diverted, the pollution caused by the sugar-gasoline mills, or the disappearance of local agriculture. "Good ethanol helps clean up the planet," said Lula. "Bad ethanol comes with the fat of subsidies. Brazil's ethanol is competitive because we have technology, fertile land, abundant water, and we are not alone. Most African, Latin American, and Caribbean countries, in addition to some Asian countries, enjoy similar conditions to ours."

Every emperor at the conference had been given five minutes to speak. Lula spoke for forty-five minutes, and the effects of his speech cannot be overestimated. From now on, energy security, food security, and economic security would be one and the same security.

In a burst of new consciousness, agrodollars became the petrodollars of the developing world. Domino's transformed a field of wheat into a pizza and then sold the pizza. But Lula expressed a new scenario and a new truth. Everyone could eliminate the product in the middle. Fields of grain equal oil, and both equal money.

8

A Short History of Wheat Futures

When I began to consider the global food crisis and the people who were trying to fix it, I harbored a bias. I figured that the field of professional hunger relief would be a ghetto for sandaled activists who spoke only of the wretched of the earth. But I soon discovered that many of those involved in food aid follow a very different gospel, and for some very good reasons.

My distorted image of the hunger activist was irrevocably shattered the third morning of the Rome hunger summit, as I sat in the back row of the Iran Room—where the United Nations held its press conferences—and listened to the remarks of Josette Sheeran, the executive director of the World Food Program (WFP). The WFP is the largest humanitarian organization in the world, part of an elite club that has spent billions trying to end world hunger. Sheeran, I realized, was the most important hunger activist in the world.

At the time of this presentation, she had just completed her first year as executive director of the WFP, and already rumor had it that she might be next in line for even bigger things at the United Nations. Sheeran was a big deal, an up-and-comer. And she was someone who looked at the bright side. "High food prices and increasing demand present a huge historic opportunity," she said. I had never considered the global food crisis as an opportunity for anything other than dying of hunger or feeding the hungry, but Sheeran was far beyond these considerations. She already understood the paradox that food was no longer about food.

As the reporters scribbled in their notebooks and tapped their laptops, Sheeran smiled. An ex-journalist, she had learned the subtleties of media relations at the *Washington Times*, the conservative daily broadsheet founded and bankrolled by the Reverend Sun Myung Moon's Unification Church, which was not only a cultish spiritual movement but a bastion of the right wing. Sheeran joined Moon's infamous church in 1975 and could boast a classic 1970s deprogramming story wherein her father, the former mayor of West Orange, New Jersey, stormed a Moonie school and tried to rescue his daughter. The attempt failed, and Sheeran remained a member of the Moonies for more than two decades, even as her spiritual leader grabbed headlines by declaring, "I will conquer and subjugate the world" and "I am your brain."

Sheeran reached a pinnacle of sorts as the managing editor of the *Washington Times*. Then, having exhausted the social, political, and professional possibilities of the Unification Church, she left the newspaper, converted to Episcopalianism, took a job as an undersecretary of state in the George W. Bush administration, and finally turned her attention to the greatest problem of all. She decided to feed the hungry.

Today, Sheeran directs the WFP's six-billion-dollar annual budget, acting as commander in chief of the WFP's vast fleets of barges, camels, donkeys, planes, trains, trucks, and elephants. The WFP is as big as international food relief gets, and since 1962 it had been collecting agricultural surpluses and sending them across the world as part of a concerted effort by the U.S. government to promote the economic interests of its farmers— not to mention the various political goals of U.S. foreign policy.

Now, Sheeran declared, the WFP was facing the biggest challenge in its history, and if her organization and the famine relief industry in general did not take immediate action, the number of hungry people in the world would soon double. "The bottom billion will become the bottom two billion," she warned. It was the 1970s all over again. By percentages, as bad as hunger could be. By real numbers, beyond the beyond.

When Sheeran finished her remarks, I followed her out of the Iran Room and asked if she could explain what she had meant when she said, "High food prices and increasing demand present a huge historic opportunity." Where was there room for opportunity in high food prices and increasing demand? Were high food prices not driving riots and famine across the globe? Were there not more hungry people than ever before? "There was a time when we did not know how to produce enough food in the world," Sheeran said, and gave me a dazzling smile. "Now we do." Of course, after half a century of providing food for the hungry, the WFP knew that the hungry needed more than food. And every hungercrat at the Rome conference understood that there was more than enough food for everyone on Earth, even if the fact of food paled before the privilege of eating it.

Within minutes, Sheeran and I were joined by her second in command, Nancy Roman, the WFP's director of communications. She observed Sheeran the way campaign managers monitor their candidates. "This is not your grandmother's food aid," Sheeran said, as Roman kept watch.

In the early days, according to Sheeran, most of the contributions that landed in the lap of the WFP came in the form of food, but as the years went by, a growing proportion of the contributions came in the form of cash. Originally, the hunger relief organization had focused on delivering its rice and beans directly to those who had the bad luck of inhabiting the most cursed spots on Earth. But as global grain surpluses went down and the price of shipping went up, the WFP took the logical step of purchasing food from sources closer to the malnutrition and famine, in many cases even from within the borders of the affected country. The year before Sheeran's speech at the Food and Agriculture Organization (FAO) conference, the WFP had purchased 19,800 tons of corn and beans from Rwanda, for $6.3 million, and 230,000 tons of food from Uganda, for $55 million. That made these countries' respective presidents, Paul Kagame and Yoweri Museveni, happy to cooperate with the WFP's designs for the future.

In fact, the WFP's plans called for the presidents of Rwanda and Uganda to travel to New York just a few months after the Rome hunger summit. There, at U.N. headquarters, Presidents Kagame and Museveni would help inaugurate the WFP's newest anti-global-food-crisis program. And on that morning, Sheeran revealed, the African presidents would be joined by the world's third richest man, Bill Gates.

Gates, a crown prince of virtuality, had reached the conclusion that given the right data, the right algorithm, and the right inputs, world hunger would be a relatively simple equation to solve. Gates, Sheeran explained, was going to help the WFP expand its program of purchasing food from small-scale farmers and grain traders in the farthest reaches of its client nations. Such purchases, as logistically difficult as they might be, would increase and support the agricultural efforts of these so-called smallholders, who would not only be equipped with fertilizers, herbicides, irrigation methods, and superseeds. This time around, the smallholder would get market savvy. "This," said Sheeran, "is the next wave of the story."

If the global food system demands that all farmers grow as much product as possible with the smallest overhead possible and with as much new technology and sophisticated accounting practices as possible, then the best way to help the poorest farmers would be to change their business models. The poorest farmers would surely benefit from shaping their small, tradition-based businesses into something more along the lines of a big knowledge- and technology-based business. And what more direct and simple and sure way to succeed in business than to sell more goods at a higher price?

So instead of delivering food, the WFP had decided to deliver the price of food. If it purchased grain from smallholders and local traders, it would put cash into the hands of hundreds of thousands of poor people and encourage small-scale farmers to plant more, harvest more, and bring more food to the market stands. Thus could a poverty-stricken farmer move from being a recipient of food aid one year to creating a bit of surplus the next, to making a profitable business out of it a few years down the line, and supplying food for others.

Since money had become the key to the hunger problem, the key to the hunger solution could be summed up in one word: markets. Many had tried to bring markets to the impoverished before, but no one had had the support of Bill Gates. And under Sheeran's direction, the WFP would *guarantee* a market where none now existed. It would do so, in part, by deploying a grain-buying tactic that dated back more than a hundred years: the WFP would promise to purchase a certain amount of a farmer's output at a certain price for one, two, or three years. Such guarantees, known as *forward contracts*, would give small-scale farmers the incentive to plant more acreage, since they were guaranteed an eventual sale—not to mention an agreed-on price—for their harvests. A WFP contract might even help farmers to get credit from the local bank or perhaps a bit of crop insurance.

Sheeran called her program P4P, which stands for Purchase for Progress. The seventy-six-million-dollar program would be funded by the Howard G. Buffett Foundation, the Bill and Melinda Gates Foundation, and the government of Belgium. In its first year of forward contracting, P4P would commit the WFP to purchasing forty thousand tons of food from 350,000 small-scale farmers. "We are studying a proposal with Bill Gates on a way to do the contract," Sheeran told me.

The goal of P4P may have been to support the smallholders, but the program itself had been designed to mimic the
most sophisticated of global financial markets. Along with its
purchase guarantees, P4P included plans to support countrywide commodity exchanges, which the WFP hoped would
develop along the lines of the world's leading derivatives mar-
ketplace, the Chicago Mercantile Exchange. Why shouldn't
small peasants get a slice of the potentially lucrative global
commodities pie? In Ethiopia and Uganda, noted Sheeran,
exchanges had already opened.

The strategy made some sense. Behind the food lay politics; behind the politics lay the money, and behind the money
lay the markets. In the WFP's latest effort to end world hunger, the smallest-scale farmer could benefit from the biggest
market. One of the biggest markets on Earth was the global
commodities market, which also happened to be the way the
world's largest food producers and processors and retailers
bought and sold their inputs, from oil seeds to oil.

Commodity exchanges are markets in which people buy and
sell derivatives. I had heard the term *grain futures* plenty of
times but had not realized until that evening that a *future*
is a financial derivative. In fact, the first market exclusively
devoted to financial derivatives was a market in food.

A grain future is in many ways similar to the infamous
derivatives that ripped apart the world's financial fabric in the
first decade of this century. And a wheat future is in many ways
similar to its twin without italics, the general term that indicates
that which may or may not happen tomorrow or next year, that

which may or may not ever exist. I had not understood until that evening in Rome that a wheat future did not refer to real and present wheat, but wheat that might or might not appear some time next month or next year. A wheat future referred to future wheat. And like the *future* future, the grain future was ever and always a mental, not a physical entity.

The wheat future did not emerge from the soil. It was fashioned by the imagination. Much as the food activist Michel Pimbert had asked the antiglobalists to *imagine* the end of world hunger, nineteenth-century American capitalists had *imagined* the grain future—and changed the world.

Why was imagining the future essential to Sheeran and the WFP's plan to end world hunger? The most basic answer was that in the Garden of Eden ever ripe fruit hung from low branches. But ever since Adam and Eve got kicked out of paradise, or Hades abducted Persephone, or whatever mythology you prefer, food has been seasonal. Unfortunately, our need to eat is not seasonal. Every day, everyone should consume two to three thousand calories. Therefore, food is all about next week, next month, and next year.

One of the first solutions to the problem of ensuring future meals was wheat. Ten thousand years ago, the ancient peasant farmers who lived along the Fertile Crescent domesticated the genus *Triticum*, and remnants of their prehistoric grains still sprout among the hills of Iran, Iraq, Lebanon, and western Syria. Early on, the farmer-scientists had discovered that wheat can be crushed into a nourishing dust, an easily stored, easily transported substance that can be styled into a multitude of forms—from matzo and baguettes, to pita and cookies and bagels, pasta, pizza crust, crackers, and hard biscuits that can last a long, long time. Before humans invented the wheel, they invented flour.

Another result of our perennial need for a nonperennial product—that is, food—is that sophisticated import and export markets in grains (not to mention copper, gold, silver, and weapons) date back to the ancient world. These markets depended on commercial promises, etched with a stylus in clay, for the future delivery of goods. A long-term contract for the delivery of ancient farro or durum meant that the grain that would eventually be delivered might not even have been planted when the promise to deliver was first made. That covenant etched in clay, much like the pledges the WFP would make to the smallholders of the developing world, was a promise for grain to be bought and sold months or years after the tablet had been marked. The cuneiform concerned grain that might exist on its due date—or not. The notches outlined promises about imaginary grain.

Civilization, as most people understand the concept, depends on populations of city dwellers, and since city dwellers cannot as a general rule supply themselves with their own food, they must purchase food from somewhere else that someone else has made. City people depend on affordable daily bread, but the price they pay for it must keep a lot of other people in business, from grain wholesalers and millers to bakers and grain deliverers, not to mention those who farm. As it turned out, many wonderful results came from buying and selling imaginary future grain, and the most wonderful result of all had to do with setting a price both buyer and seller could count on and budget going forward. Imaginary grain helped stabilize the price of actual grain.

The modern history of the price of rice began in 1730, when enlightened bureaucrats of Japan's Edo shogunate perceived that a stable rice price would not only protect those who produced and consumed their country's sacred grain but also align with the country's national interest. Ever since rice was bought and sold, all of the farmers in Japan brought their crop to market after the September harvest, at which point warehouses would overflow, prices would plummet, the rice market would tank, and for all their hard work, Japan's rice farmers would remain impoverished.

Instead of suffering through annual rounds of volatility on the Dojima rice exchange in Osaka, the bureaucrats decided to set a price that would ensure a living for farmers, grain warehousers, the samurai (who were paid in rice), and the general population—a price not at the mercy of the annual cycle of scarcity and plenty but a smooth line, gently fluctuating within a reasonable range. It was a civilizing moment, this vision of value that spanned space and time and generated a price that would guarantee satisfaction for both buyer and seller.

The Osaka rice market illustrated one of the most important laws of food. When the price of food halves, we do not consume double the amount. When the price of food doubles, we cannot wait until it drops to buy more food. And while consumers of cars and television sets may postpone the purchase of a Honda or a Sony, food consumers cannot postpone the purchase of breakfast for a month or a year.

In the technical parlance of the economists, food markets possess *low elasticity*. But the Dojima rice exchange was a market that did not lose sight of the fact that the commodity being bought and sold was not simply a widget but a product that meant life itself to the Japanese people. For food is not like other commodities. No matter what the supply, demand remains the same.

• • •

By lucky happenstance of climate, the central region of the United States offers ideal conditions for growing grain. Wheat loves cold winters and moderately dry springs, and as urban U.S. populations blossomed throughout the nineteenth century and store-bought bread became a household staple, ever more massive wheat harvests meant ever more massive cash sales. The cash, in turn, became the lure for more settlement of the Midwest, which meant more farmers in the wheat business, which meant more wheat, more bread, and more money.

A new class of Great Lakes grain entrepreneurs created lucrative new trade routes to deliver their wheat to the markets of New York City by way of the Erie Canal and the Hudson River. And by the middle of the nineteenth century, enormous warehouses in Buffalo, Milwaukee, and other major Great Lake ports began to construct their own versions of Joseph Dart's 1842 invention, a steam-powered bucket-belt that could hoist endless loops of grain to the upper stories of grain depots and empty a ship in a day.

The grain elevator, as it was called, meant that more wheat than ever could be translated more quickly into more dollars than ever, which attracted the attention of the East Coast banking elite. And as mid-nineteenth-century wars stirred up mid-nineteenth-century political turmoil for Britain, France, Russia, and Turkey, hunger flourished across Europe. It was U.S. grain that came to the rescue, and as the grain went global, so did dollars.

There was so much money in *Triticum* that throughout the Midwest, cash and wheat became synonymous. This identity of a virtual measure of value (such as cash) and a real, nonmetaphorical substance (such as wheat) does not happen often in economic history, but it does help to define the term *commodity*. What was money? Wheat was money. And it could be traded as such.

But the first great boom in U.S. grain busted in 1856, when the Crimean War came to an end and Russia returned to the business of exporting wheat from the Volga River basin. "This year the Europeans do not want our breadstuffs," ran an editorial in *Harper's Weekly*. "They have a surplus at home." The price of U.S. grain plummeted, and the commodity crash was followed in quick succession by more general economic and financial disasters: a credit crunch, bank runs, a stock market collapse, and a recession.

When the so-called Panic of 1857 had run its course, U.S. grain merchants conceived of a new way to combine dollars and wheat into something that could be bought and sold, and that something had everything to do with imagining the future. Unlike the Japanese rice system, the U.S. wheat system did not set prices. Instead, buyers and sellers would sign forward contracts to deliver or accept grain a few months down the line, on the expiration date of the contract, at a negotiated price.

Of course, neither the nineteenth-century wheat-buying grain merchant nor the nineteenth-century wheat-selling farmer could predict droughts, floods, freezes, or weevils, so neither the buyer nor the seller could be certain what the going rate for wheat would be on the eventual date of the promised delivery. As a result, the agreed-on price of a future bushel of wheat usually rested a few cents below that of a bushel of wheat presently on the market. And while farmers had to accept less for future wheat than for real and present wheat, the guaranteed future sale protected them from the disaster of collapsing prices. The future prices were guesses, but they helped both the wheat seller and the wheat buyer to manage the innately risky business of farming and milling, and in so doing reduced the volatility of the price a city dweller paid for a loaf of bread.

Like the grain-trading system that had originated in the Dojima rice market, the forward contract system was beautiful in theory and practice. These new food derivatives helped to feed millions of city dwellers, for the prices of forward contracts for wheat that did not yet exist always *derived* from the present prices of wheat that did exist (hence the term, *derivatives*). But the forward contract, for all its merits, was a primitive financial tool.

The Civil War, like the Panic of 1857, changed the way wheat got its price. In the economic boom that followed the war, the demand for wheat exploded, and ever-increasing numbers of grain merchants took to reselling and rebuying forward contracts on a fast-growing secondary market. But the forward contract had not been constructed to change hands so many times, more like money and less like food. The more traffic in forward contracts, the more impossible it became to figure out who owed whom what and when. At which point the great grain merchants of Chicago, Kansas City, and Minneapolis set about creating a new kind of institution, less like a medieval county fair and more like a modern clearinghouse. They founded what we know today as the grain futures market.

Under the forward contract system, every buyer and every seller had to know and trust and sign an agreement with whoever stood at the opposite end of each deal. But the new grain exchange would serve as the counterparty for every buyer and seller. In other words, once the grain exchange accepted you as a market participant, you could buy or sell grain on the exchange and not have the slightest idea whom you were buying from or selling to.

And in place of huge numbers of individually negotiated and fulfilled contracts for the delivery of a specific quality of future wheat on a particular day in the future, the exchange regulated both the quality of grain and all the expiration dates of all forward contracts—eventually limiting the grain contracts to five each year, in March, May, July, September, and December. Every stake in future wheat had to be taken for one of those five contract delivery dates. And instead of limiting trade, the regulations proved liberating. "It is a great reform," declared a report from the New York state senate. "It will never go back."

The trading of U.S. wheat futures, pioneered by the ancestors of what we now know as "Big Ag"—the presidents of Archer Daniels Midland, General Mills, and Pillsbury—helped to establish the United States as a financial juggernaut to rival and eventually surpass Europe. And the new market created the occasion for so many people to make so much money in so many ways that numerous other futures exchanges soon opened, featuring contracts for the future price of everything from Golden Delicious apples to butter, cottonseed oil, hay, plywood, poultry, raw silk, rubber, and cat pelts. Futures exchanges sprung up in Buffalo, Cincinnati, Dallas, Duluth, Houston, Indianapolis, Louisville, New Orleans, Omaha, Peoria, St. Louis, Toledo—and the list went on.

Before World War I, New York City had seven commodity exchanges operating full tilt, which meant that if a speculator who traded molasses futures on the New York Coffee and Sugar Exchange lost his shirt, he could head over to the New York Burlap and Jute Exchange or the New York Hide Exchange. Speculation in cat pelts came and went, but grain futures weathered the Great Depression, and after World War II the United States was routinely producing grain surpluses, which became an essential element of Cold War political, economic, and humanitarian strategies. Not to mention the fact that U.S. grain fed millions of hungry people around the world.

And despite the occasional market collapse (onions, potatoes) and the inflationary run of the 1970s, the price of wheat generally remained stable, farmers made a living, food processors made a killing, an increasing number of people had plenty to eat, and, generally speaking, the United States prospered.

In fact, the exchange-based pricing system that worked so well for U.S. grain has proved durable and underpins the structure of today's six-hundred-trillion-dollar global derivatives business. Futures markets now range from Ethiopia to Cambodia, Nepal to Karachi, Vienna to Sydney, Bratislava to Minneapolis, Atlanta to Zhengzho. These exchanges no longer trade molasses and burlap, but they do conduct business in oil and gold, corn and coffee, natural gas and nanomaterials, livestock and biofuels, diamonds, plastics, rubber, and carbon emissions. The Chicago Mercantile Exchange recently created a weather futures market, in which the participants can bet on future hurricanes, frost, and snow.

But the first modern futures market was a grain futures market, and the first financial derivative was derived from food.

• • •

Bill Gates of the Bill and Melinda Gates Foundation and Josette Sheeran of the World Food Program had decided that their solution to global hunger would include commodity markets. This was a clever tactic, because almost everyone at the 2008 FAO meeting had agreed that the food problem required some sort of cash solution.

But not all cash is created equal. In fact, there are two specific kinds of cash that people invest in grain futures, and these two kinds of cash come from two different categories of investors, and these two investors possess different goals and, subsequently, pursue two different kinds of results. The problem is that no one can tell one kind of money from the other.

From the outset, grain markets have included *hedgers* and *speculators*. The hedgers are the farmers, the millers, the bakers, and the warehousers, the investors in food who have a stake in food. The corn growers in Iowa and the wheat farmers in Nebraska participate in the grain futures market as hedgers, along with major multinational corporations like General Mills, Pizza Hut, Kraft, Nestlé, Sara Lee, Tyson Foods, and McDonald's—companies whose publicly traded shares rise and fall on their ability to bring affordable food to peoples' car windows, doorsteps, and supermarket shelves. These participants in the grain market have been called bona fide hedgers, because in order to conduct their core business, they actually need to buy and sell a great deal of cereal.

Bona fide hedgers consider the grain futures markets as risk-management tools, because the exchanges provide a practical way for farmers and food producers to gather a sense of how much money they will be getting or spending at different points in the future. Buying and selling futures contracts helps hedgers hedge the risks of an inherently risky business.

But the word *hedge* brought me up short. Like the word *derivative*, *hedge* has had to bear a great deal of pressure in recent years, mostly for its presence in one of the hallmark financial phrases of our time, the hedge fund. And just as I had started out with no understanding of commodity markets, I'd had no idea what the *hedge* in *hedge fund* meant. Before I could get a fix on the two kinds of investors who power the commodity markets, I had to look into the hedge.

Way back in the year 785, just around the time the Vikings began to ransack northern England, the word *hedge* entered Old English. A hedge defined any man-made boundary, the basic demarcation of property and ownership, the philosophical line between what is mine and what is yours. Five hundred years later, when the word had migrated into the lexicon of Modern English, the economic and philosophical line between "mine" and "not mine" had waxed militaristic, and the definition now included arsenals of physical defense: hedges of archers, spears, or stick-wielding police. At which point in linguistic history, one man's hedge became another man's extreme bad luck.

Yet another half a millennium had to pass before hedging matured into gambling. In 1672, *hedged bet* first appears as a phrase, with an implication of shaky moral standing. The hedged bet was for knaves, and Shakespearean English abounds with hedge wenches, hedge cavaliers, hedge doctors, hedge lawyers, hedge writers, hedge priests, and, what may be worst of all, hedge wine.

The first evidence of investor hedging appears in 1723 in the coffeehouses of London's exchange alley, where caffeine-addled proto-brokers bet on the movement of equity stakes in the Bank of England, the South Sea Company, and the East India Company. Investors who owned shares in these companies could offset the possibility of future losses by hedging, which meant betting in advance on the stock's downward movement. A hedge had become a way to assure yourself of a win no matter which way a wager came out.

But it wasn't until 1928 that the *Saturday Evening Post* defined the word for use on Wall Street: "hedge clauses . . . signify that if the representations turn out to be wrong *the banker shall not be held accountable*" (emphasis added). Twenty-one years later, the first Wall Street hedge fund was born. At which point hedging had been firmly established by more than a thousand years of social, political, military, literary, and linguistic history as another way of saying, "Heads I win, tails you lose."

A hedger must be crafty, but even more crafty must be his traditional counterpart in the futures markets, the speculator. And what is a speculator? Up until my interest in food commodities, I had considered speculation the occupation of philosophers. To speculate was to engage in reflection, to conjecture, to theorize. Speculation implied thinking, not doing, for in order to speculate, the speculator must take a step back and contemplate phenomena from a distance. Speculation, like the word *spectacles*, implied a certain kind of enhanced vision, and in *The Wealth of Nations* (1776), Adam Smith acknowledged the economic advantage of seeing what others could not see: "Sudden fortunes, indeed, are sometimes made . . . by what is called the trade of speculation."

Speculators in the futures markets make their money through the most traditional of all profit-making tactics: the art of buying low and selling high. While bona fide hedgers possess a real physical stake in grain, speculators neither produce nor consume corn or soy or wheat, and they wouldn't have a place to put the twenty tons of cereal they might buy at any given moment, if ever it were delivered. The salient attribute of the grain speculator is that he or she makes (or loses) money without ever touching grain. To the speculator, the grain is wholly imaginary. Only the money is real.

Recently, speculators in grain have come to outnumber hedgers in grain, which means that there is more imaginary grain bought and sold on the futures exchanges than actual grain harvested from the earth. But on the exchanges, it doesn't matter if the wheat is real. What matters is the price. For the grain on the futures market is future grain, grain that does not yet exist, a grain *derivative*, a virtual form of food.

Now we are getting a little ahead of ourselves—the grain futures business is a complicated business. Of course, it is the complication that keeps people who are interested in food away from the onerous details that define the price of food. So let's just say that on the futures markets, hedgers and speculators work together to "discover" the price of wheat.

They do not always necessarily work at cross-purposes. In fact, the hedgers—the farmers, the warehousers, Nabisco, Kraft, Pillsbury, Pizza Hut, McDonald's, and the rest—welcome speculators to their market, for an endless stream of speculative buy-and-sell orders fills the futures market with money. The money the speculators use to buy and sell allows the hedgers to sell and buy just as they please. And since buying and selling grain allows the hedgers to manage their risks, speculation in grain futures is essential for hedging grain futures. At least, that is the theory.

Of course, one might argue that the whole thing is a theory. A clearinghouse in which hedgers and speculators buy and sell imaginary future wheat in order to stabilize the price of real and present wheat depends on a wide range of abstract concepts and assumptions. But if you have stuck with this short history of U.S. grain and the different kinds of people who buy and sell it, there are only one or two more theoretical tidbits to digest. One of these has to do with a term created in the twentieth century, an expression especially invented for the futures markets. The term is *normal backwardation*, and it was coined by the British economist John Maynard Keynes.

Every day across the United States, grain growers, grain processors, and grain warehousers buy and sell wheat at the *spot price*, which means the real price a real buyer pays a real seller of real wheat on the actual premises of a farm or a silo or a grain depot. While the spot price of wheat is set any day or time a buyer and a seller agree on a price, the price of a wheat future settles only on its contract date, and there are only five contract dates, as mentioned earlier: in March, May, July, September, and December. When a future contract settles, it becomes, for all intents and purposes, no longer the future but the present—which means that the price of the futures contract should, at the moment it expires, equal the real, present price of wheat. As a futures contract expires, its price should equal the spot price.

Every ten weeks or so, as the delivery date of the upcoming futures contract approaches, the general rule is that hedgers and speculators take their profits and losses. They clear their promises to buy or sell with equal and opposite promises to sell or buy, and as they do so, the spot price of wheat and the futures price of wheat gradually converge. The virtuality of future wheat adjusts to the reality of present wheat, and the price of an ideal bushel is revealed.

Keynes, the most influential economist of the twentieth century, applied himself to the study of this miraculous interplay of supply and demand, present and future, real and imaginary. He modeled the interdependences and called his model normal backwardation because in a normal market for real goods, he found that futures prices (for things that did not yet exist) generally stayed a little less than the spot prices (for things that actually existed). I would certainly spend more for a chocolate bar I can eat right now than for a chocolate bar I may or may not eat three months down the line. Normal backwardation is common sense.

But let's say you don't want to buy or sell any chocolate bars—or any corn or soy or wheat. Let's say you just want to make money in the futures market. That would mean you are a speculator, and as such you head to the wheat pits of the Chicago Mercantile Exchange and note that the nearest wheat futures contract stands at six dollars a bushel. You could buy a *promise to buy* a bushel of wheat for six dollars on this nearest contract date, but you have done a great deal of research and have it in your mind that wheat is overvalued at the present moment. So, instead of buying a promise to buy wheat, you buy a *promise to sell* wheat on the nearest contract date for six dollars a bushel. Then you go home and get some rest.

Of course, the price of the wheat contract you bought into fluctuates minute by minute on the big board of the Chicago Mercantile Exchange, and the next day, when you return to the wheat pit, you find, to your delight, that you were correct in your assessment of the market. Wheat was overvalued, and consequently the price of your wheat futures contract has fallen to five dollars a bushel. At that point you decide you'd like to take your profit. So you buy (for five dollars) the bushel of wheat (entirely imaginary) that you previously sold (for six dollars)—and earn yourself a dollar for your troubles.

It does not matter that you never had any wheat to sell in the first place. You have escaped any and all contractual obligations to deliver or receive a bushel of real wheat by canceling your first promise (to sell) with an equal and opposite promise (to buy). You have made a dollar by correctly perceiving that wheat was overvalued and the price of the futures contract would fall. In the parlance of the grain exchange, you have "gone short" on wheat. You have bought low and sold high, although not necessarily in that order. You have made a profit through the ancient art of speculation.

It was this sort of thing that Bill Gates and the WFP believed could end world hunger.

9

The Food Bubble

The next morning in Rome I opened the newspaper to discover that food riots had erupted a few hundred miles to the north. On June 3, in front of European Union headquarters in Brussels, police armed with shields and batons had charged hundreds of protesting fishermen from France, Italy, Portugal, and Spain. The Associated Press reported that as the protesters retreated down the main boulevard, they "broke into EU buildings, smashing windows and dragging out flags and other items to burn in the street." Next to the AP story, the *International Herald Tribune* reported that Monsanto had announced a new generation of seeds that required almost one-third less water than ordinary seeds and promised to double yields for corn, soybeans, and cotton.

I opened the *Financial Times* of London and discovered that billionaire investor George Soros was painting a bleak picture on commodities and was now calling the high prices of corn, wheat, and oil a bubble. "Misplaced investing in indices by institutions is to blame for soaring valuations," he noted. I thought this was an interesting article.

Soros was saying that something had gone wrong with the commodity markets. The price of food was higher than it should have been. The balance of hedgers and speculators had been lost, normal backwardation was out the window, and the ingenious interplay of the real and the imaginary on the futures exchanges could no longer stabilize prices.

Soros was not saying that the soaring price of food would make farmers, food processors, or even food retailers rich. Nor was he saying that the rising price of food had anything to do with better-quality food. Soros was saying that something had gone wrong with the market for food futures. And he was implying that someone somewhere was making boatloads of money. Of course, that someone, somewhere, didn't necessarily have anything to do with meat or potatoes. Perhaps that someone was a new kind of speculator in financialized food, someone who had figured out a new way to pump money from the derivatives of our daily bread, the cost of which was rising at unprecedented rates.

Such surges in price are called bubbles. In 1841, Charles Mackay wrote a book called *Extraordinary Popular Delusions and the Madness of Crowds*, in which he described one of England's first financial bubbles, the so-called South-Sea Bubble of 1720. "The populace are often most happy in the nicknames they employ," wrote Mackay. "None could be more apt than that of bubbles."

It was 2008, and there was a food bubble. I put down the papers and gazed at the Circus Maximus. "It is most unjust that the hunger of one's own fellow-citizens should be a source of profiteering for anyone," the Roman consul Antistius Rusticus had lamented two thousand years ago—but nobody listened to him.

I walked past the ancient chariot track and headed over to Mussolini's old headquarters, where I had scored an interview with Nancy Roman, the World Food Program director of communications and public policy strategy. She and the WFP executive director, Josette Sheeran, went way back. When Sheeran had been managing editor of Reverend Sun Myung Moon's *Washington Times*, Roman had been Sheeran's congressional bureau chief.

Before Roman joined the fight against world hunger, she had been president of the G7 Group, a political and economic research and advisory firm, and had made her living explaining Washington policy to hedge fund managers. As a result, Roman could situate virtually any political or social phenomenon within easily comprehensible financial constructs. She could explain why, in the midst of rocketing world food prices, the Ospraie Special Opportunity Fund and the BlackRock Agricultural Fund had gone on their latest buying sprees, snapping up grain silos, grain elevators, fertilizer distribution centers, and huge tracts of land—not to mention some serious stakes in grain futures contracts.

Wall Street understood value, but Wall Street didn't get Washington policy, Roman told me. But as the world's best and brightest in New York, Washington, and Rome had begun to focus on global food security, the solution to the age-old problem of hunger appeared increasingly to coincide with the age-old techniques that the best and the brightest themselves employed to ensure their own security. Money would solve the problem—money sunk into arable land, fresh water, and commodities all the way up and down the line. The solution to the global food crisis was more investment, and all investments, noted Roman, were speculative.

I asked her to tell me more about the plans of Purchase for Progress, funded by Belgium, Warren Buffet, and Bill Gates. If investment was the solution to world hunger, what kind of offer was P4P making?

The WFP could not always purchase a peasant's grain as soon as the harvest came in, explained Roman. Instead, the WFP would encourage farmers to warehouse their grain in exchange for a receipt. More mysterious than rice or millet, this slip of paper presented a number of intriguing possibilities, for the receipt allowed the farmers to register with their countrywide commodity exchange, a place in the capital city where all of the grain from all of the country's farmers could be bought and sold. Henceforth, farmers could follow prices with the technology of their cell phones. The once indigent smallholders could become commodity traders and peg their sales to any time of the year. And so the farmers might forecast, model, and even leverage more financing.

No matter that commodity speculation had just been implicated in the world food crisis. No matter that two months before the FAO conference, the Agribusiness Accountability Initiative had declared that massive and unregulated grain trading had "pushed the prices of wheat, maize, rice and other basic foods out of the reach of hundreds of millions of people around the world."

Of course, the WFP could take no responsibility for market peaks, valleys, doldrums, and crashes. The happy news was that the solution to world hunger would no longer have to be about food, science, or politics. It could be about the fluctuating price of grain on commodity exchanges. The solution could be all about the money. And to this end, the farmers-turned-traders could hold their grain receipts as long as they liked before they decided to sell their grain, and while they waited they could place bets on which way the market would move. They could hoard in the great tradition of grain dealers, hedge in the great tradition of hedgers, speculate in the great tradition of speculators, and eventually pull in enough profit to render obsolete every guarantee and support of the WFP, quit farming, and go into insurance and banking. And I imagined the sowers and reapers of Africa, Asia, and South America—the impoverished billions transformed into a massive cartel of grain dealers to rival the great Cargill and Archer Daniels Midland—leveraging, diversifying, and driving up the price of rice and beans.

This reminded me to ask Roman about rising food costs, food bubbles, and all of those riots erupting across the planet. "I'm not a purist," she said. "As a capitalist, things can go wrong. But I think part of what is happening that is good is it's got to be worth someone's while to fix these problems."

I thought that was a strange response. Roman, like her boss, Sheeran, believed that rising food prices presented some sort of opportunity. Perhaps, in the near future, it would be "worth someone's while" to fix the problem. After all, food was getting more valuable by the minute.

"People say, how long will this price thing last? Well, I don't know," continued Roman. "Rising for the next couple of years. Not coming off below 2005 levels before 2017. So this is like a midrun problem, we think."

A midrun problem, I reasoned, could offer some midrun opportunities. Higher farm prices could conceivably help farmers; higher grocery bills could conceivably benefit packagers and retailers. Speculation in commodity markets could be a boon for investors of all shapes and sizes. But how did the financial fluctuations affect the urban underclass of Nigeria, the rural poor of Guatemala, and those who pushed the vegetable carts of Sidi Bouzid? Not to mention the hungry people of Los Angeles, Chicago, and New York. "Listen," said Roman, "speculation always drives up the cost of everything—housing, telecommunications, shoes. I'm a humanitarian who believes that capitalism works. But you see investors where they think some demand will be. They're going to make money on it, the market develops, and that could help the world."

Her voice trailed off and we gazed at the muted, closed-circuit image of yet another head of state. "What people are uncomfortable about is when you speculate about food," said Roman, "something so fundamental to life. When you're speculating on something that is the essence of life, when you're speculating in that space"—and here she stopped. She gazed across the press room, and frowned. "People don't like that," she concluded. "For agriculture to work in Africa, guess what we need? Roads, storage, and technical expertise. And that takes money. That takes investment." She lowered her voice. "I've been saying for some time the world needs an Internet-like breakthrough in agriculture."

The higher the price of global food, the more persistent the dream of the killer app. If only grain could follow the lucrative footsteps of software and social media and mimic the venture capital successes of technology. Roman knew that a number of lucrative innovations in virtual food had already been made. Perhaps it was only a matter of time before we could jettison the physical act of farming.

I remembered a conversation I'd had before I left for Rome. The food activist and New York University professor Marion Nestle had warned me against intoxicating visions. Investment in global food, Nestle said, should not be devoted to bioinformatics, neutraceuticals, and next-wave technological flavors of the week but should focus on the basics: women's education, clean water, and sanitation. "But there's no money in it," she had said.

Nancy Roman, on the other hand, dreamed the dream. "Who knows what science can do?" she said. "Seeds that don't need water would be great."

Then she recalled her more sensible side, and the pragmatic language of the hedge emerged. "You've got a long-term demand pressure [that is, hunger]," she explained. "People are saying that this [i.e., food] is going to be valuable to the world—and they're right. Is there going to be a point of discomfort [that is, starvation]? A hundred percent there is. You're in the discomfort zone right now, and it is uncomfortable to be in this space. It is a scary place, but these high prices are driving innovation. And we cannot be afraid."

I asked her if she ever got to New York. She would be there in the fall, she said, when Bill Gates came to address the United Nations.

It was the last day of the Rome hunger conference and the hottest new investment was not Apple, IBM, Facebook, sovereign debt, or a short sale of mortgage-backed securities. The hottest investment was land that could produce feed for pigs and cows and cars, land that could deliver bread to the stomachs of vast swaths of humanity, bread that could keep people fat and happy in their homes, not rioting in the streets. The hottest new investment was land wherever in the world it happened to be undervalued, from Brazil to Burundi. Hundreds of billions of dollars, euros, riyals, and yuan were sinking into the jungles of Ethiopia, Mali, and Mozambique.

The Chinese and the Saudis had purchased foreign water rights, while the BlackRock Agricultural Fund, the Braemar Group, Emerging Asset Management, and a host of other hedge funds had made plans to sow and reap whatever plant or grain would prove most fruitful profitwise. More than military might, more than oil, food security meant financial security. "Investors Pour Billions into Farming," read the that morning's headline of the *New York Times*.

That afternoon, I headed back to the Iran Room for a Q&A with Donald Kaberuka, a Rwandan economist who has been the president of the African Development Bank since 2005. He was a bald man with thick glasses, and his group had just announced a billion-dollar donation to the FAO. "We absolutely must ensure the markets are working," Kaberuka said as the cameras flashed and videos rolled. "We encourage more private investment. There is everything to be built."

I asked Kaberuka about the article in the *New York Times* that morning, the piece that had reported hedge and sovereign wealth funds buying immense tracts of land in sub-Saharan Africa. Did the African Development Bank support such purchases? Was it at all concerned that investors might abandon their properties if and when the commodity did not yield the forecasted results? "Let me be very clear on this one," said Kaberuka. "The time has come for African agriculture to become a business. We welcome all inflow of private investment."

Late in the afternoon of the final day of the High-Level Conference, one of the most anticipated news conferences featured former U.N. secretary-general Kofi Annan. The human rights champion, born in Ghana, had earned his master's degree from the Massachusetts Institute of Technology's Sloan School of Business and had risen through the ranks of the United Nations until he became its head. As part of his duties, Annan had traveled to the World Economic Forum in Davos and delivered a speech in which he called for a "global compact" and "creative partnership" between the United Nations and the private sector, a bond that would unite the Earth's human population, the Earth's environment, and the Earth's biggest businesses. Annan had called for a union that would, in one quotable phrase, "give a human face to the global market."

In 2001, Annan received the Nobel Peace Prize. "We have entered the third millennium through a gate of fire," he noted in his acceptance speech. "A new insecurity has entered every mind." Seven years later, the old insecurity was back, and so was Annan. He had come to Rome to sign a document that would officially establish an organization of organizations called the Alliance for a Green Revolution in Africa (translated into UN-speak: AGRA). The goal: an end to food insecurity on the most food-insecure of all continents.

AGRA consisted of a dizzying array of chieftains, presidents, and deputies of the FAO, IFAD, WB, and WFP. FAO, of course, stood for the Food and Agriculture Organization of the United Nations, headed by Jacques Diouf, the Senegalese diplomat desperately in need of $30 billion a year to end the global food crisis. The WFP was the World Food Program, led by Josette Sheeran. IFAD stood for the International Fund for Agricultural Development, an agency the United Nations had organized in response to the food crises of the 1970s, the crisis that the technocratic fixes of the Green Revolution had stalled but not stopped.

WB was the World Bank, whose president, Robert Zoellick, had held a number of positions under Presidents Ronald Reagan and George W. Bush. Zoellick had also served as international vice chairman of the investment bank Goldman Sachs and had long been a champion of markets without borders. But the food bubble of 2008 was testing Zoellick's resolve. He may have sat placidly smiling on the dais, but the ever escalating price of the world's food and a billion hungry people had turned his vision of free-flowing international markets into a dispute among nationalists, each of whom was aggressively executing policies to tamp down the price of food for their own people while enforcing tariffs and trade barriers for everyone else.

The only one not yet onstage was AGRA's chairman of the board, Kofi Annan. The press was waiting.

Behind the last row of seats, a line of television cameras balanced on tripods, and as the huddled masses of scheming *journalisti* pushed into the little theater, so did the buzz of prime-time hunger—transnational media, topic-A, try-to-spin-it-your-editor's-way hunger. This was just the kind of hunger extravaganza the FAO publicity pack had labored for months to achieve: stuffed-pressroom, *carabinieri*-guarded, media-credentialed and security-checked hunger, attended to by hordes of harried interns and crimson-blazered, perma-smiling FAO staff.

This was Nobel Peace Prize hunger, private-reception hunger, bedizened and be-flagged, flanked and branded by baby-blue FAO logo. Here was hunger tailor-made for the TV standups in their heels and makeup, ready for starvation Q&A. Here was hunger all gussied up in its ancient royal regalia, ready to seduce column inches from the *New York Times* and Reuters and *Newsweek* and the BBC. This was scramble-for-your-seat, silver-pitcher-of-iced-water-on-the-desk, video-streaming, closed-circuit hunger. High-Level Hunger. No hungry people in sight. Everyone could smell a story.

Nick Parsons, the FAO's communications director, mounted the pulpit and stood before the crowd. Resplendent beneath the klieg lights, he gazed at his BlackBerry. Next to Parsons stood the FAO's Italian head of security, who glanced at the *carabinieri* and raised an eyebrow. It was time.

Kofi Annan—former secretary-general, Nobel laureate, card-carrying global elder—was marching onto the dais. The video rolled, the still photographers unfurled a downpour of flash, and the world's assembled press delivered the ultimate sign of respect: silence.

Nick Parsons turned on the microphone. "This is a particularly important event," he said. A few sentences later he sat down, and FAO chief Diouf stood up.

"Ladies and gentlemen," said Diouf, "I am pleased to welcome you to this ceremony for the signing of this Memorandum of Understanding."

In FAO-speak a Memorandum of Understanding was an MoU—to be signed by IFAD, WB, and WFP—all of which would ceremonially inaugurate AGRA, which the Bill and Melinda Gates Foundation had already favored with $264 million.

"The world is witnessing an unprecedented global food crisis," said Diouf. None of the assembled press made note. That was old news. "In Africa, the situation is particularly deep-seated," continued Diouf. Still no pen touched paper. "More investment is needed."

Eventually the FAO leader took a seat and Kofi Annan stood and strobes of camera flash lit the Iran Room. The AGRA chairman made his way through the disco lights to the microphone and began to deliver a speech, but somehow the sound system in the Iran Room had at this extraordinarily inopportune moment managed to malfunction, and no one could hear what Annan was saying, a fact that made no difference whatsoever to the photographers, who kept flashing madly, but made Nick Parsons frantically pantomime to the audience that we should listen through the headphones. Despite the fact that no one could hear what Annan was saying, after he finished saying it he was rewarded with a crushing wave of applause.

Annan sat down, Josette Sheeran stood up, and the microphone began working again. "Solutions to hunger cannot happen by governments and UN agencies alone," said the head of the WFP. "So I think the creation of AGRA—and the combined talents of the Gates and Rockefeller Foundations—is good news for the world's most vulnerable. Today we have experienced a revolution in food aid."

Then Sheeran began to explain P4P, which rested on one basic principle. If you can't bring farmers to the commodity markets, bring the commodity markets to the farmers. The market, the miraculous mechanism whereby grain got its price—that was the answer to the world food crisis.

The *carabinieri* scanned the crowd. "Now," said Parsons, "I'd like to ask the principals to sign the memorandum on behalf of their organizations"—at which point the assembled hunger fighters brandished their pens and the photographers elbowed to the front of the room. Finally, at long last, here was some news: the moment hunger ends. Annan fiddled with a blue ballpoint, laid it down on the white tablecloth, extracted a gold pen from his breast pocket, and signed. Then Parsons opened the floor to questions.

"Does the memo you signed today have any significance more than symbolic?" asked the correspondent from the Arabic Service of the BBC. "What will happen this afternoon? Tomorrow? Next week? What will happen in tangible terms?"

Sheeran replied that dollars from Gates had already provided salt iodization technology to Senegal. "This is a revolution in cooperation," she said.

"AGRA is training African scientists," Annan added—and this time the microphone worked. "We have breeding going on. We have better seeds, which will produce a much higher harvest. We are working with an equity bank, giving a guarantee of five million dollars, leveraged to fifty million dollars, to make fertilizers available to the farmers in Kenya." At that point someone shouted a question from the back of the room: Would genetically modified crops be part of the plan for Africa?

The silence settled as we waited for the verdict on proprietary technology, AGRA's stand on food as intellectual property. Everyone hoped that African food markets would increase African food supply, but would Africa's agricultural markets be the next great opportunity for monopolized meta-food? Everyone on the dais knew that Africa possessed many of its own varieties of rice, along with native millet and other less famous grains such as fonio, sorghum, and teff. Dozens of other wild species had developed over tens of thousands of years, each adapted to survive the stresses of heat and drought. Did such second-class cereals face oblivion in the face of borderless megafood?

Annan chose not to answer the question.

Outside the Iran Room, the dog and pony show had hit full throttle. A dozen television reporters flapped in unison, each famine narrative vying for its ninety seconds of media supremacy. Drowned out by the newscasters, consigned to one of the lowest rungs of the hunger narratology, Jim Marurai, Prime Minister of the Cook Islands, had been given this time slot to address his fellow emperors. The Cook Islands are a smattering of fifteen South Pacific volcanoes and reefs situated somewhere between French Polynesia and American Samoa, and as far as I could tell, no one cared what the prime minister had to say. As far as I could tell, no one cared about the Cook Islands and Marurai's "serious concern" that his little republic of corals, ash, and atolls was sinking into the sea. "What sort of world have we become when we can receive images from cyberspace at an incredible speed into a device that can be held in our hand, yet so many of us are not able to download the nourishment we so badly need into our bellies?" asked Marurai.

Meanwhile, those members of the press with the nastiest deadlines paced among the potted palms of the FAO's glass-roofed vestibule, desperate to intercept the hungercrats as they slunk across the red carpet from one side of Mussolini's building to the other. "There's no news," complained Phil Stewart of Reuters. Paddy Agnew of the *Irish Times* had a potato famine lead for his article, and that was it. Barbie Nadeau, the Italian correspondent for *Newsweek*, sat next to me in the press room with her reporter's notebook open. Her weekly magazine was demanding precisely 120 words on the Rome solution to the global food crisis. A hundred heads of state and three days of conference would be relegated to a couple of paragraphs.

And then there was Richard Owen, the veteran from the *Times* of London, famous for scooping the state dinner menu from the previous high-level hunger conference, thereby bringing to light the scandalous fact that the assembled Excellencies, after vowing to halve the number of starving people in the world by 2015, had feasted on lobster and foi gras.

Owen had ferreted out the emperors' menu this time, too: vol-au-vent with sweet corn and mozzarella, pasta with cream of pumpkin and shrimp; veal olives with cherry tomatoes and basil; fruit salad, and vanilla ice cream, all washed down with a Vin Orvieto Classico Poggio Calvelli. So far, that was the most e-mailed story from this world hunger conference—along with the shoe-shopping spree of Zimbabwe's First Lady, Grace Mugabe.

Majid Chaar, the FAO's chief of media relations, was delighted with the way things were shaping up. "There are fifteen hundred journalists here," he told me. "Three hundred television outlets. And the pledges . . ." He raised an eyebrow.

As I chatted with Chaar, a hunger lobbyist came up and whispered that I should have been at the farmers' press conference. Ah, yes—the people who still think it's about food. I had not realized the peasants had sent a contingent. Didn't they realize they were out of the picture, that food was now cash?

For just as money had begun the conference, money ended it. A frenzy of pledges marked the final hours of the summit, although no one at the conference really understood what would be done with their money. Ed Schafer, the U.S. secretary of agriculture, led the charge with an announcement that the U.S. Department of Agriculture would donate five billion dollars over the next two years. President Nicolas Sarkozy announced that France would throw in one billion euros. "Dying people are not happy people," he noted.

After Sarkozy's pledge, IFAD announced a gift of $200 million. The WFP mobilized $750 million, and the World Bank pledged $1.2 billion. Kaberuka's African Development Bank threw in their $1 billion. Spain pledged $773 million; the United Kingdom, $590 million; Japan, $150 million; Kuwait, $100 million; Venezuela, $100 million; the Netherlands, $75 million; New Zealand, $7.5 million; and the Islamic Development Bank, $1.5 billion.

"For what?" whispered one hungercrat I met in the hallway. "It is unclear."

After the final spasm of pledging, the only thing left was to ratify the conference's official declaration, which consisted of the conclusions the previous emperors had ratified more than a decade before, give or take a few statistics. The entire assembly would ratify the document paragraph by paragraph, so I prepared for a long evening of debate and deliberation by heading upstairs to the FAO's Polish Bar and downing a few shots of Mexican tequila. By the time I returned to my spot in the white Formica press ghetto, I was surprised to discover that the emotional condition of the political assembly had already declined to a state of numb fury. Debate was deadlocked.

The paragraph that had caused the uproar read, in its entirety, "We will strive to ensure that food, agricultural trade and overall trade policies are conducive to fostering food security for all. For this purpose we reaffirm the need to minimize the use of restrictive measures that could increase volatility of international prices."

What to do about the price volatility of global food? That was the question. Were more markets, and more open markets, the answer to prices that swung out of control, or could sovereign states dictate their food imports and exports as they wished, no matter what the price of world grain, no matter who might be starving? The emperors had zeroed in on the word *restrictive*.

FAO president Diouf recognized the representative from Venezuela, who indicated she would like to make a brief statement. Perhaps the word *brief* had been mistranslated by the U.N. interpreters, for the statement turned out to be an extremely long and convoluted declaration of extreme regret that a wonderful opportunity to terminate the scourge of world hunger had deteriorated into yet "another example of world domination." Certain countries, noted the Venezuelan representative, were "imposing their dominion." Everyone knew whom she meant.

Relations between the United States and Venezuela had been tense since the 1998 election of the Venezuelan president, Hugo Chavez, whose tenure had been marked by statements such as "I hereby accuse the North American empire of being the biggest menace to our planet" and "Capitalism leads us straight to hell." In fact, two months after the FAO hunger conference closed shop, the Venezuelan president expelled the U.S. ambassador from his country, closely followed by the reciprocal expulsion of the Venezuelan ambassador in Washington.

After the Venezuelan representative sat down, it was time to hear from Zambia, the landlocked southern African country where two-thirds of the citizens do not have enough to eat. "I think the issue of hunger and poverty is not one that should be subjected to semantics," said the Zambian delegate.

Five years before, the U.N.'s Zambia National Human Development Report had declared: The fight against poverty and hunger will determine whether Zambia joins modern and progressive nations of the 21st Century or she is relegated to the dark ages, her people continuing to suffer deprivations that should long have been consigned to the pages of history.

"In the spirit of unity," continued the Zambian delegate, "in the spirit of those who are dying, we want to recommend that the text be ratified en bloc."

Unfortunately, a number of others disagreed with the Zambian assessment. What better time to air political tensions than during a debate about hunger? Dozens of delegates' hands reached toward the sky. Diouf, still dressed in those flowing blue robes, recognized Cuba.

"The aggressions of the United States to Cuba have not avoided manipulating food as economic and political pressure," noted his Excellency, Señor Don Enrique Moret Echeverría, the Cuban delegate. "We continue without finding truly sustainable solutions to the problem of hunger. The rich and the powerful continue to block that."

Bolivia came next: "I just wish to express Bolivia's support of Argentina, Venezuela, Cuba, and Nicaragua."

And so it went. The FAO cleaning women wiped the traces of coffee and candy from the tables. One by one, like injured soldiers hobbling back from the front, the press abandoned Mussolini's old palace. The new story had become the old story. Dinnertime came and went.

10

Let Them Eat Cash

Not too long after the Rome conference, I met Nancy Roman for breakfast at the Affinia Dumont Hotel in Midtown Manhattan. As I waited in the lobby for the World Food Program's director of communications, I relaxed in an overstuffed chair and watched virtual food shimmer across the wall. An ornate picture frame surrounded a wide-screen television that glowed with images of carrots, kale, lemons, oranges, peppers, and spinach. Interspersed among the fruit and vegetable close-ups and fade-ins flashed snippets of text: "Be well" . . . "Eat the pulp" . . .

Mesmerized by the food that wasn't there, I did not notice Roman walk up until she said hello. She looked different from how she had appeared in Rome: a bit more tired, a bit less hopeful. She had just returned from Ethiopia, she told me, where she had toured a number of small villages. She did not go to the northeastern province of Wollo, the site of the great famine of the early 1970s in which tens of thousands of herders and tenant farmers had starved to death. Instead, she traveled south, toward the Kenyan border, where the drought had been intensifying and where the WFP had constructed a stabilization center.

"People could barely stand," she said. "The children were swollen with edema and listless." And when Roman had asked how people were coping, a man grabbed a clump of grass from the dry dirt. "This is what we're eating," he said.

A woman had told her, "We hate our children now."

"It's beyond heartbreak," said Roman.

We sipped our lattes. "We're just repeating history," she said. "We all feel it's such a special moment in time, but no. It's happened in every generation."

The standard reaction of the Roman plebe in times of food shortage was to surround the emperor's palace and threaten to burn the grain-hoarding senators alive. When severe food shortages struck during the Middle Ages, merchants set up stalls in the open market and purveyed chops and steaks of human meat. During eastern Europe's great hunger of 1032, parents sold their children.

Above the anecdotes towered a chronicle written in 499 by a Christian monk, Joshua the Stylite. Only one copy of the manuscript exists—in the Vatican library—but scholars have translated the grisly tale from ancient Syriac into German and English. Nancy Roman had just read it. "I shall tell presently to the best of my ability," began Joshua, "though no one, I think, could describe it as it really was."

The events Joshua described took place in Edessa, an ancient city fifty miles east of the Euphrates River, close to the present-day border of Turkey and Syria. "Locusts came upon us out of the ground," wrote the monk, "so that the very air was vomiting them. They ate up and desolated and utterly consumed everything."

Edessa's food supply dwindled, and the prices of wheat, chickpeas, and lentils spiked. "Children and babes were crying in every street," observed Joshua. "Of some the mothers were dead; others their mothers had left, and had run away from them when they asked for something to eat, because they had nothing to give them. Dead bodies were lying exposed in every street. Others cut pieces off corpses, that ought not to be eaten, and cooked and ate them." Even after Emperor Anastasius I relieved Edessa of its tax burden and distributed money to the poor, the price of food continued to rise, and the famine did not end.

"It could have been a conference at the United Nations," said Roman. "It's the same basic food commodities we're dealing with today. Lentils, chickpeas. And shortages caused by the same thing. And the other thing—they're distributing cash, which is what we're thinking about in urban areas. Distributing cash."

The waitress took our order, and Roman began to tell me about the behind-the-scenes negotiations with Ethiopia, where food reserves are perennially low, prices are perennially high, and nine million people are hungry. Roman, it appeared, was a skilled envoy and had come from the Horn of Africa to New York City to iron out the details of yet another top-secret matter of hunger diplomacy. "I'm negotiating a deal with a celebrity to be a spokesperson for hunger worldwide," she told me.

Veteran press handler that she was, Roman would not reveal the identity of this celebrity. But as food riots continued to erupt across the planet, the moment had arrived to augment Drew Barrymore's one-million-dollar donation made a few months earlier, live on *The Oprah Winfrey Show*. There was some urgency here, for a mighty cash deposit from another household name would be perfect preliminary public relations for the main event, the sixty-nine-million-dollar World Food Program/Warren Buffet/Bill Gates Purchase for Progress extravaganza coming up in a few months at world headquarters of the United Nations, just a short cab ride from where we sat at the Affinia Dumont. That sixty-nine million dollars would inaugurate the forward contract–creating, warehouse receipt–providing, commodity-trading, market-based solution to the global food crisis. I planned to be in the audience on that historic day.

Which was when it occurred to me that I was a part of Roman's press strategy. For what other reason would she have met me for breakfast? Certainly not to discuss edema in Ethiopia and the chronicle of Joshua the Stylite. It was Roman's job to hit guys like me over the head so I would publicize the WFP. It would take a lot of famine narratives for magazine readers who had plenty of pizza, french fries, and soda to come to grips with other people's hunger.

"Bettina just had a big break with a celebrity," said Roman. Bettina Lüescher, the former CNN international anchor, was the WFP's senior public affairs officer. "We have more celebrities coming to us," continued Roman. "The moment is coming. There's energy behind it. This really could be our time. This could be hunger's moment."

I nodded and smiled, but I doubted that this would be hunger's moment. In the long sweep of starvation, many such moments had come and gone. And the history of hungry people was generally interrupted but never eclipsed by the history of rich and famous people coming to the rescue—be they Drew Barrymore, quarterback Joe Montana, sportscaster Erin Andrews, or ancient Greeks like Apamea, Epidaurus, and Megalopolis. The Greeks had a word for the public display of generosity. They called it *euergetism*.

Even way back when, almost everyone understood that donations would not be a lasting solution to the problem. Then again, it was possible that P4P would succeed where *euergetism* had failed. Perhaps Gates, master of the pragmatic, would know how to transform virtual food back into something real.

P4P was an attempt to end world hunger by means of communications technology, futures markets, and Internet guruship deployed across some of the nastiest spots on Earth. It was unclear if the tactic would work. But the approach reminded me of my visit to Domino's world headquarters. J. Patrick Doyle and his crew were not simply rearranging the deck chairs on the *Titanic*. They were using math and science and business school analytics to find the very best way to rearrange those chairs, to sustain the unsustainable. They were certainly meeting some measure of success, but that didn't mean the project was successful.

In Niger, following a spate of local purchases like those promised through P4P, millet prices actually rose by 13 percent in local markets, followed by a 7 percent national increase. Guaranteed food sales had increased consumer prices, which sent more people into poverty and starvation. The gift of cell phones and forward contracts had triggered all manner of unforeseen consequences. And when drought hit Niger two years later, the warehouses promptly emptied, and eight million people faced food shortages.

What could have caused such reversals in world food when the system had futures markets, global pizza, sustainability quotients, transgenic chemistry, transnational gifts, and *euergetism* of every sort? I couldn't begin to answer this question without talking to a man named Amartya Sen.

When Sen was nine years old, he witnessed the Bengal famine of 1943, the last of a long line of British-supervised Indian famines, which occurred only four years before the end of British rule. Between two and three million people died, and Sen had watched them drop in the streets. This was the famine that occasioned Winston Churchill to remark during a 1943 Cabinet meeting that the catastrophe was of no great account because the Indians would simply "breed like rabbits."

When Sen grew up, he became a university professor. His specialties included the economics of poverty and famine, and many of his 26 books and 375 articles deal with these subjects. For much of his academic career, Sen has focused on the fact that during the worst period of the Irish famine of the 1840s, "ship after ship sailed down the Shannon, bound for England, laden with wheat, oats, cattle, hogs, eggs, and butter." In other words, during the famine there had been plenty of food.

Similarly, during the Ethiopian famine of 1973, food moved out of Wollo Province and headed toward the tables of more affluent purchasers in the capital, Addis Ababa. Such uncanny food countermovements during food shortages led Sen to the insight that if governments were to intervene in such situations, famines would not be very difficult to prevent. "The rulers," he noted, "never starve."

Sen had crunched the hunger numbers as no one else had done before, not just for Bengal in 1943 and Ireland in the 1840s but also for the Ukraine in the 1930s, China in the 1950s and 1960s, Bangladesh in 1974, and Somalia and Sudan several times over. In 1982, his book *Poverty and Famines: An Essay on Entitlement and Deprivation* transformed the field of development economics. Other books followed, including *On Ethics and Economics* (1987) and *Inequality Reexamined* (1995). In 1998, Amartya Sen was awarded the Nobel Prize in Economics.

He lives in one of those quaint shingle-style houses a few blocks from Harvard Square, close by the gates of Radcliffe College and the Episcopal Divinity School. The coffeehouse down the street offers a sandwich called "Mr. and Mrs. Snob," and the bookstore next door overflows with the immortal ruminations of deep thinkers.

I found Professor Sen dressed in an Oxford button-down, a gray sweater vest, a pair of khakis, and baby-blue socks. He was writing a letter to an old friend on a laptop next to the couch, the computer held up by eight volumes of the *Encyclopedia Britannica*, half of them still in their cellophane wrappers.

First we ate; then we talked. His daughter served baked fish in mustard seeds, and after lunch, since Sen was recovering from surgery, we retired to the living room and he reclined on the pink couch, a yellow coverlet tucked under his chin, his head and his knee propped up on an elaborate arrangement of seven pillows. Next to him sat a pitcher of ice water, a bottle of Evian, a box of Kleenex, a pair of crutches, two phones, and two assistants.

"When people think they believe in this or that," said Sen, "I'm not sure." He paused for an enormous amount of time. He moved the pillows, straightened the coverlet, and glanced at the two watercolors that hung above the fireplace, portraits of Willard Quine and John Rawls. "They were close friends," he said.

Quine and Rawls had once been the anchors of Harvard's philosophy department. They had argued that in order for truth to be true, it had to be grounded in the world. People who were hungry and the ideas about people who were hungry could not exist in separate realms. Neither could food and virtual food.

As we looked at the portraits, it occurred to me that Sen was not a modern economist as much as a philosopher, which was what economists used to be before dogma and divination got in the way. The solution he had found to world hunger had been the outcome of an extraordinarily acute and rational analysis of the facts at hand, the same approach René Descartes had employed to cast a cold eye on the nature of his own existence, the same methods Socrates had used to face death without flinching.

"I believe in reason," said Sen. "There are those who want to repress reason. Christian, Muslim, and Hindu fundamentalists, and those who pick a totem market economy, the liberal economic state. These are all antireason."

According to Sen, markets exist to serve people, not the other way around, and it was unreasonable to worship a market simply because it was a market. Men and women created markets, just as we carved idols, composed hymns, and wrote prayers.

Sen paused and closed his eyes. I knew he had written the introduction to a book on AIDS in India that had been funded by the Gates Foundation, and I wondered if the affiliation would cloud his perspective, but after a few minutes he began to expound on the relationship of market-based movements of food to demand and purchasing power, and he explained that none of these forces necessarily had anything to do with who gets enough to eat and who doesn't.

In fact, there was no fixed relation of any sort between food and famine. Some famines, like the one in Bangladesh in 1974, occurred in years of peak food availability. And in the midst of a severe hunger crisis, agricultural subsidies do not make much of a difference, he told me. Nor do superseeds or take-out pizza. In the face of famine, a reliance on market economies is as ineffective as a reliance on loaves and fishes or manna from heaven.

Despite the postsurgical codeine, Sen was sticking to his talking points, the narrative of his great insight: famine is not about not enough food. Which was great news. If hunger has little fixed relation to what can stop hunger, then famines should not be so terribly difficult to avoid.

The solution: speedy implementation of emergency income and employment programs, in combination with the broader social infrastructure of representative democracy and a free press, which happens to be the best early warning system. No matter how many farmers hold warehouse receipts, own cell phones, or trade grain futures, hunger will happen where there is no free press. Even more often, famine will happen where rulers are alienated from those they rule. Sen explained that a functioning democracy is a simple way to remove such alienation. "It's not easy to win an election after a famine," he said. And rulers tend to feel embarrassed when photographs of starving children appear on the front page.

Problem is, there's money to be made on food—and the less food, the more money. The problem is that the markets do not exist to increase flavor, boost health, or fill every empty belly. The markets exist to set prices and maximize profits. Today's innovations are market innovations, and we can bet they will be tomorrow's innovations, too. For innovations in prices and profits must evolve.

But the answer to the food crisis is already with us. Sen had discovered the elements of the solution and had gone over them many times, in abstruse tables for the journal *Econometrica*, in articles for the *Handbook of Mathematical Economics*, and in features for the literary magazine *Granta*. He had explained the antidotes to hunger in his hundreds of essays and two dozen books and in thousands of seminars and public addresses, yet his endlessly rehearsed points had not been enough. The world remained irrational, and people starved.

Now, more than three decades after the publication of *Poverty and Famines*, hunger analysis had shifted its focus, and there were those who whispered that Sen was outdated. Authoritarian governments could stop famine and malnutrition just as easily as representative democracies, some argued. Private philanthropy was making a comeback. The global food-market fix was just getting started.

"There is no one solution," Sen said. "Any solution will have to be a complex bundle, and no one organization can do it. None of the organizations alone can."

I asked if the U.N. Food and Agriculture Organization was up to the job.

"No," he said, and closed his eyes. "That I profoundly doubt."

What about Bill Gates and the World Food Program?

"It can do a lot of good," Sen said. "But it's not the way of solving the problem."

I broached the topic of the United Nations and his friend, Kofi Annan.

"He always knew what to say," said Sen. "And even more important, what not to say."

Then I asked the kind of question I thought one was supposed to ask a Nobel laureate, the biggest big-picture question I could imagine. Were things getting better or worse?

Sen looked at me and said, "It depends where."

The time had come to ask Bill Gates a question.

The United Nations had convened its Sixty-Third General Assembly, which meant block after block of river-view highrises cordoned off by riot police, gunships patrolling the East River, frogmen in the water, helicopters in the sky, SWAT units in SWAT vans, waves of incensed demonstrators from China and the Upper West Side, and a rainbow coalition of dark-suited, grim-faced, crewcut, heavyset men who spoke into their lapels.

Past the police barricades the climate-change, bioenergy, and hunger crowd had magically reappeared—the same presidents, prime ministers, and assorted excellencies and thugs I had seen in Rome, in addition to a new entourage whose identity badges read BILL GATES DELEGATION. Among the representatives of 192 member states, the presidents of Rwanda, Tanzania, and Uganda may have been the happiest of all to see this new delegation.

And so I found myself winding through the U.N. building's underground maze of baby-blue barricades, mini-militias, and metal detectors until I reached conference room 4, one of those vast interiors that promised the future of the world in its bold angles and curves and molded plastic chairs bolted to the floor. The burly guys with automatic weapons were not letting anyone in until the K-9 unit had given the all-clear, so I loitered beside a huddle of WFP underlings who snapped to attention when Nancy Roman marched into their midst, followed by their executive director, Josette Sheeran.

When the hounds headed out, the press headed in. We dispersed around the great modernist semicircle of egalitarian unidesk, and I settled less than ten feet from the big nameplates on the elevated dais. Presidents Yoweri Museveni of Uganda, Paul Kagame of Rwanda, and Jakaya Kikwete of Tanzania flanked to the right of the empty chair for Gates.

Museveni had been born a peasant, and Kagame had spent his youth in Ugandan refugee camps, his family exiled from one makeshift city to another, from Tooro and Rukinga to Gahunge. Now they would share the stage with a billionaire.

Kikwete's grandfather had been a Tanzanian chief, so he may have felt a bit more comfortable than the others in the presence of such power. When Kikwete came to the United States, he would often make the business media rounds, visiting the headquarters of NASDAQ and the set of CNBC to tout his country as an international investment opportunity. But as business with Shell, Dominion Petroleum, and

De Beers increased, Tanzania had veered into what the International Food Policy Research Institute was calling an "alarming level of hunger."

There was a lot at stake for the three African presidents. P4P not only meant money for each country's largest grain producers, it also meant money to establish each country's national grain futures exchange, which opened up a wide range of new opportunities for hedging and speculating on food. The developing world's grain exchanges would require experts in grain derivatives, which meant experts in the field of "grain banking," which meant experts in markets, which meant people who knew how to handle great loads of cash.

There are a number of technical details that make grain exchanges a potentially lucrative business for those who run them. For example, in order to act as the clearinghouse for every order to buy or sell a grain future, a commodity exchange must hold some money from each trader, known as the *margin requirement*, as an ante to get into the commodities betting game and to cover possible losses. These deposits make the exchanges look very much like banks.

The larger the exchange, the more money for the bank that holds the margin requirement. Of course, those responsible for the margin requirements could conceivably leverage this money into even greater sums of money. And the more speculation and hedging, the more volatility and arbitrage, the more daily winners and daily losers, the more money required to cover the margin. The more money required to cover the margins, the more cash on hand.

Now Bill Gates and Josette Sheeran walked up to the dais, deep in conversation, and the photographers' flashbulbs lit up her red dress and his yellow paisley tie. Silence settled as

Bettina Lüescher, the WFP's senior public affairs officer, took her spot off to the side of the stage and thanked everyone for coming. "This is a wonderful event," she observed. Then she introduced her boss.

Sheeran welcomed everyone to the kickoff of P4P, then got right to the point. "Today you see a partnership determined to put hunger out of business." Sheeran recited her litany of ever worsening facts and figures, including the latest hunger statistics, which indicated that the number of malnourished people had gone up once again and the cost of fertilizer in some areas had risen 400 percent. "Farmers are reeling," she said.

ActionAid International, a global antipoverty organization, had just released a report noting that a full quarter of the world's population was now being denied its "right to food." Droughts in Australia and Ukraine had destroyed harvests. In Nigeria, the price of *gari* had doubled. Authorities in Bihar, one of India's poorest states, suggested that everyone switch from eating rice to eating rats. "Eating of rats will serve twin purposes," Vijay Prakash, an official from the state's welfare department, told Reuters. "It will save grains from being eaten away by rats and will simultaneously increase our grain stock."

As Sheeran continued from where she had left off in Rome, Gates began, as is his custom, to rock in his chair, his eyes fixed somewhere in the middle distance. He rocked and picked his ear and nodded and grinned, and eventually he turned on his microphone. "It is an honor to be here with this group," he said. He looked down the table and nodded at the African presidents, who nodded back.

Then, in the great visionary tradition of the United Nations, Gates spoke of a world in which the problem of rats and the rising price of *gari* might be solved if only the haves could educate the have-nots. This time the lesson was about markets. "Ultimately, the goal here is to have these markets be self-sustaining," he said, noting that most of the world's poor people happen to be farmers. "Allowing them to participate in these markets is a real win-win."

The speech was short, but just as in olden times, the richest of the rich had made a point of his largesse. When classical Athens descended into one of its periodic food shortages, long-forgotten, deep-pocketed celebrities like Xenokles and Archestratos bestowed hundreds of thousands of *medimnoi* of grain upon the suffering city-state and made things right. The ancient celebrities were rewarded with bronze statues, names carved in marble, and front-row seats at the games. This morning at the United Nations, it was euergetism all over again, and the African dignitaries knew the drill.

"Let me join Josette in expressing my sincere appreciation for Bill Gates," said President Kikwete. "It is our problem," he continued. "You are coming to our rescue."

Kagame was the next African president to speak. Out of a population of nine million, almost five million Rwandans are at risk of going hungry, and Kagame, the Tutsi general who had dominated his country's politics since his forces ended the genocide of 1994, was on his best behavior. For President Kagame understood the importance of commodities. Since the 1930s, when the Belgian colonial government began to require that Rwandan farmers plant coffee trees, coffee had been one of Rwanda's most important cash crops. Today, Starbucks sells a lot of it. But in 1989 the global commodity price of coffee collapsed, the Rwandan economy shook, Hutus began killing Tutsis, and a civil war erupted.

"We are very happy in Rwanda to be associated with this program," said Kagame. "It is our duty as governments to make these cooperative efforts work."

Kagame then yielded the floor to Uganda's president, the elder statesman of the little group. "High food prices are very good for us," said Museveni, who had been criticized for arresting opposition leaders, clamping down on the press, and working to destroy some of the last remnants of Uganda's rain forest in order to reward politically connected plantation owners for whom high food prices were indeed a very good thing.

In northeast Uganda, more than seven hundred thousand people did not have enough food. In the provincial capital of Moroto, three-quarters of the population were starving to death. But even in this region, escalating prices for beans, cassava, maize, and sorghum had not stopped the commercial development of jatropha plants—exclusively for biofuel extraction.

"Thank you, Josette," concluded Museveni. "She buys a lot of food from us," he said. "And I salute Mr. Bill Gates."

Lüescher returned to the microphone and asked if anyone had any questions. I raised my hand, but she called on someone else. Second question, she looked right past me. Ditto for the third.

"We are running out of time," said Lüescher. "One last question."

She gazed at the multitude of hands from front to back and all around the arc of the majestic semicircle. Then she smiled and said, "Fred."

I clicked on my microphone and said I had a question for Mr. Gates: Despite all he was doing to end world hunger, might not programs like Purchase for Progress in the end perpetuate market conditions that actually promote world hunger?

An uncomfortable silence settled on the room, and for the first time that morning Gates stopped smiling. Instead of answering my question, he asked one in return; the only indication of his annoyance the fact that he forgot to turn on his microphone. "What do you mean by 'market conditions'?" he asked.

I had planned my question in advance, but never suspected I would be required to speak at any length. Now I found myself in front of a microphone, in full possession of my own famine narrative, a story that had been accruing for months, if not years. An irresistible urge took hold, and I launched into the tale of ancient Roman mobs rushing the royal palace, Joshua the Stylite, and medieval markets for human flesh and living children. The history of the world was the history of hungry people, I declared. Money, politics, war, Demeter, Hades, Domino's Pizza, Tyson Foods, genetically modified rice and tomatoes—none had been enough to stop starvation. And so on and so forth. Josette Sheeran sat frozen behind the dais.

More money did not mean better food for more people, I went on. The food system was better at filling the pockets of the rich than the stomachs of everyone else. Every dollar that entered the system was more likely to end up in the profit statement of a multinational corporation than in the pocket of a small-scale farmer. How could his money change any of that?

Gates scowled. "You should track what the food output has been," he said, and this time he remembered to turn on his microphone. "The amount of food being produced in the world today is much greater than millennia ago." His face had grown red as he gazed down from his perch beside the African presidents. "Incredible progress has been made," he insisted. "You get operating markets, they can feed the world very well. This money is being spent because it improves the human condition." And now his smile returned. "If you look at historical figures and do not see a positive trend, you might not choose to be involved. But I do see a positive trend."

Gates shook his head and turned off his microphone, and Lüescher announced that the news conference had come to an end. At which point Jakaya Kikwete switched on his microphone.

"To assume that what the assistance that Bill Gates and Howard Buffett are extending to African farmers is doing is perpetuating hunger," said the president of Tanzania, "that is a big misconception." The idea that Gates, the WFP, and the global market might actually be increasing famine would interrupt the virtual food factory headed Kikwete's way: his fertilizer market, his seed market, his loans, his futures-and-options technology, his commodity clearinghouse, and all the financial leverage that would come with his slice of progress pie. And so Kikwete recommenced his well-rehearsed paean to the new era of hunger management.

"I am seeing a lot of sense in what they are doing," he said, but no one was listening anymore, not even Lüescher, who called above the growing chaos in the room that the news conference was over. The press moved forward, shouting questions in a fruitless quest to extract something more from Gates, who ignored the noise. Tanzania's chief executive still would not stop. Kikwete wanted his money and his markets, and he would keep talking until he got them.

After fifteen minutes of screaming and yelling, the aides and the secretaries cleared the room and everyone in it, including the WFP crowd and the Gates delegation. I retreated through the high-security maze to the open air of the U.N. plaza, where camera crews blew cigarette smoke into the sky.

I strolled through the flower garden for a bit and stopped before an enormous bronze statue. Three titanic ship masts rose from a freighter packed with hordes of refugees. The ship had been moored in the grass of the U.N. sculpture garden, and a great bronze crowd of dispossessed were disembarking—a haggard, impoverished, hungry miscellany, blinking at the shore and all it promised. These were the proverbial starving masses, some covered in rags, others shirtless, their rib cages etched in metal, their hollowed-out eyes chipped into their suffering faces, their stomachs concave.

For millions of years, *Homo sapiens* flocked across continents in pursuit of bird, beast, and fresh water in the never-ending hope that there might be some place hunger did not exist. As I looked at the bronze, I remembered the words of Laurent Sedogo, the U.N. representative from the impoverished African nation of Burkina Faso, who had traveled from Ouagadougou to Rome to attend the FAO's High-Level Conference on World Food Security. I had listened to Sedogo's five-minute speech through headphones.

The speech made none of the news reports, none of the blogs, and none of the live satellite feeds. Perhaps no one else in the world had heard Sedogo. Everyone in the political assembly upstairs had either been off buying shoes with Grace Mugabe or busy negotiating grain tariffs, taxes, and swaps to care too much about the plight of a landlocked for-mer French colony of fifteen million, a country first populated more than sixteen thousand years ago by hunter-gatherers searching for food.

But one of Sedogo's phrases had stuck in my head. "Prom-ises," he said, "have remained empty."

PART IV

Looking for Money

Cursed is the ground for thy sake; in sorrow shalt thou
eat of it all the days of thy life. Thorns also and thistles
shall it bring forth to thee; and thou shalt eat the herb of
the field. In the sweat of thy face shalt thou eat bread,
till thou return unto the ground; for out of it wast thou
taken: for dust thou art, and unto dust shalt thou return.

—Genesis 1:17–19

History . . . knows the names of the king's bastards, but
cannot tell us the origin of wheat. That is the way of
human folly.

—Jean-Henri Fabre, *The Wonders of Instinct*, 1918

11

Fresh Water and a Shotgun

For all of their market worship, Bill Gates and Josette Sheeran understood that it was not the transnational food producer, the technocrat, the academic, the scientist, or the politician who stood at the base of the global food crisis. It was the tiller of the soil: the peasant.

I thought peasants were a thing of the past, so I was surprised to discover the number that exist today. More than a billion of them still till the soil. In the strange vocabulary of development economics, they are called the smallholders: the men and women (the majority of the world's small-scale farmers are women) who cultivate a few acres, most often pay rent for the privilege, and, who, by virtue of their number, manage to feed more than half of the people on Earth.

Paul Freedman, the chairman of Yale University's history department, has considered the question of the peasant for years, and on a rainy summer afternoon we sat on the chintz couches of his Westchester home, drank a few beers, and discussed the turnip eaters of Germany, the pea eaters of France, and Shakespeare's mule-headed Bottom, a peasant foolish enough to woo a goddess. "Peasants were not human so much as objects," Freedman told me, "filthy and stupid objects that deserved contempt." Peasants were coarse, comic, cowardly, deformed, gullible, ignorant, lazy, and ugly. Like Shakespeare's Bottom, they were no more than mules.

Then came the backlash. A few hundred years ago an idea sprung up that the cursed cultivator of the soil might be ennobled by the sweat of his brow and even end his humble career closer to God than his evil oppressors. Cursed in the past, might not the peasant be blessed in the future? And could the blessed peasant redeem the world?

Freedman explained the new stereotype, the virtuous peasant, nourishing of society, clever, resourceful, simple, pious, and unlearned. Think of Thomas Jefferson's gentleman farmer, Leo Tolstoy's soul of nations, men and women who were God's special concern. The peasant-mule had become a peasant-prophet, the sentimental ideal, the poetic rustic familiar to readers of Lord Byron, Samuel Taylor Coleridge, John Keats, and William Wordsworth—bucolic, innocent, and in possession of untold stores of unlearned, natural wisdom.

But that was not the end of the story, said Freedman. When the earlier version of the peasant (cursed, stupid, lowly) eventually resurfaced and merged with the later version of the peasant (heroic, blessed, wise), the resulting hybrid terrified polite society. Here was yet another stereotype: a righteous, rebellious, violent peasant, hell-bent on apocalypse or—even worse—equality. So ended our first beer.

Of course, the angry, politically minded peasant paid a price. In the Peasants' War of 1525, three hundred thousand German turnip eaters fought without artillery, and a hundred thousand of them were promptly slaughtered. Freedman rattled off an unpleasant history of peasant strife in Normandy, Hungary, England, Flanders, and Catalonia. Then came the French Revolution, spurred by bad harvests, spiking bread prices, general starvation, and the phrase a young queen most likely never said: "Let them eat cake."

But no matter how reviled, revered, ridiculed, or feared the peasants of ages past might have been, no one ever argued that they were absolutely unnecessary. Until today, when transnational commodity crop growers and megaprocessors of industrial food products insist it is they, and not two billion peasants, who should fill the stomachs of the planet's mushrooming urban population.

As I listened to Freedman talk about the transformation of the peasant, I realized I had to talk to one. Of course, I could have hopped a plane to Chiapas or Lusaka or Khartoum and camped out with subsistence farmers and a case or three of bottled water for a couple of weeks, and written the last chapters of my book. I could have joined a band of migrant workers in Central Florida or the San Joaquin Valley in California and spent my days picking lemons or lettuce and my nights sleeping in a shack. I could have visited the dairy farmers of Cajamarca, and described their plight. I could have spent a season in Bihar, where the lines of exploitation were clear.

But the stories I would have gathered would have been the stories other people had already told. And even if I retold the old stories, I would not have been able to escape the peasant clichés: either simple, virtuous, and pious or angry, righteous, and rebellious.

The curse of the peasant persists in clichés. In the United States, a country that lacks a history of peasantry, the small-scale organic farmer has become a new folk hero, an ever more rarefied object of romance and nostalgia. Every few weeks, journalists feature yet another set of noble and sexy tillers of the soil. Sustainable chicken farms in Brooklyn make headlines, and slow food—that is, garlic, onions, and turnips—has become the cuisine of sophisticates and subsequently been attacked as elitist.

I sort of liked those articles about the chicken farmers in Brooklyn. I bought my fruits and vegetables and rustic loaves of bread at the local green market, believed in local and sustainable food, watered and weeded my own small garden, and felt like a noble and virtuous peasant as I plucked my tomatoes. And now Freedman was suggesting that the peasant I knew from poetry, plays, history books, the *Huffington Post*, and green markets—that this peasant was an imaginary being.

"All this hand-wringing in France about the death of the peasant is so ironic," said Freedman, "since the French spent hundreds of years being contemptuous of peasants. Only as they are being annihilated do people remember the peasant."

I needed to find a modern American peasant who was not a figment of my imagination, not the mysterious "other" of the academics, not a noble savage, not a quaint anachronism, not a romantic redeemer of the world, not the incensed

revolution-bent wretched of the earth. I couldn't find anyone who fit the bill until a friend of mine suggested I call
Sandy Lewis.

Sandy Lewis was neither going bankrupt nor lacking for food,
for he was a banker—or at least he had been a banker. Banking was in his blood. His father, a former semi-pro football
player, had run the investment bank Bear Stearns from the
1930s until 1978, and Lewis had grown up very rich and very
sickly in a very large Park Avenue apartment that reeked of
his father's excellent cigars.

Lewis left New York to attend the University of Chicago,
returned to become a Wall Street trader, founded his own
firm at age forty, and less than ten years later found himself
indicted by an aggressive federal prosecutor named Rudolph
Giuliani. It was the 1980s, and one of Ivan Boesky's insider-
trading pals had fingered Lewis in one of the multitude of
insider-trading scams that capped a decade of Wall Street
glamour and profits. Faced with fifteen years behind bars,
Lewis pleaded guilty and walked away with three years'
probation.

It may come as no surprise that the Lewis family possessed a number of influential friends, and on President Bill
Clinton's last day in office, Lewis received a presidential
pardon. It was around this time that he decided to become
a turnip eater. The ex-banker sunk what must have been a
fair bit of his fortune into twelve hundred acres in New York
State just west of Lake Champlain, and as we sat on rocking
chairs and drank coffee on his front porch one late summer

morning, he told me about the impending economic collapse of the Western world. "No matter what you do, it won't make a difference," he said. "We have finally reached the breaking point."

Lewis understood international currencies and commodity markets. He understood the technicalities of hedging and speculating, of going short and going long, and of doing both at the same time. He understood all sorts of abstruse financial derivatives and had decided in favor of something else. In fact, scores of doomsday-envisioning hedge fund managers had begun to fill out their portfolios with farmland and ranches, the cost of which was escalating at 20 percent a year. An unsteady U.S, dollar, a tanking euro, fears of hyperinflation, and increasingly precarious global politics indicated clearly what would be of value.

"It's going to come down to food, fresh water, and a shotgun," said Lewis, sounding less like a follower of Rudolf Steiner's spiritual science of biodynamics and more like a survivalist—which was, perhaps, what peasants had been up to all along. Thousands of years before the traders of Wall Street, the farmer had been the first to place the all-or-nothing bet. Firstfruits and animal sacrifices were the ancient margin calls, the primal hedge against all the starvation-inducing mayhem of wind, rain, and locusts. Without the farmer there would be no spreadsheet, no science of sustainability, no molecular biology. There would be no World Food Program, no World Bank, no Alliance for a Green Revolution in Africa, and no United Nations.

There would definitely be no markets. For the farmer was the first speculator and the farm the first portfolio. All in all, Sandy Lewis made a great peasant.

● ● ●

I asked Lewis for a tour of his wetlands and woodlands, the grass meadows on which his herds of cattle grazed, and his fields of alfalfa and hard white winter wheat. He grabbed a walking stick and brought me around back to the six-car garage, where tucked in among the rakes, hoes, and wheelbarrows was a BMW station wagon. But the BMW was not Lewis's farm-touring vehicle of choice. He preferred something with a bit more muscle to review his assets, and that would be the Porsche SUV. Soon we were careening through grasses that stretched to the horizon, accelerating past herds of organic Herefords and Black Baldies certified by the U.S. Department of Agriculture. "That's me as far as you can see," said Lewis. "You're never going to see the whole farm. It's too big."

He steered through his forests and fields and the vast cement parking garages he had built for his tractors and his plows, then hit the brakes so we could take our time to admire a pond he had constructed that was one mile around and twenty feet deep. As the water sparkled in the midmorning sun—just as the morning pond water of bucolic peasantry was supposed to sparkle—Lewis prophesied that one day his farm would be a leader in the production of organic animals of the highest quality. He was sure he would make a lot of money selling the beef from his grass-fed cattle to the cancer researchers at Dana Farber, the professors at Harvard Medical School, and the brain surgeons at Massachusetts General Hospital. "Let's give them the best meat," he said.

We pulled away from the million-dollar pond and were soon bumping and swerving through an overgrown field of tangled grass that rose above the car windows. "This is an unusual farm," Lewis told me over the Porsche's computer controls, which were now beeping in alarm. "We have no runoff."

Runoff laced with chemical insecticides and synthetic nitrogen fertilizers was the sort of thing that created dead zones in rivers, streams, and the Gulf of Mexico. How, I asked Lewis, had he managed to construct a farm with no runoff?

He told me he had sunk more than a million feet of drainage tiles three and a half feet beneath his soil. He had dug quarries and blasted rock, then crushed and excavated three hundred thousand cubic feet of granite. Then Lewis's crew began to build dams. "It's really expensive to create a farm with no runoff," he said. I asked him how expensive. He would not tell me.

On the way back to the big house, Lewis pulled up next to a clearing where he had recently installed four enormous state-of-the-art grain silos. I didn't ask him how much they cost. We watched as a farm intern from Clemson, South Carolina, stopped on her way down the side of one towering container and gave us a wave.

Anthropologists have proposed that prehistoric warehouses stuffed with the primitive ancestors of barley, rice, or wheat may have enabled small, insecure tribes of hunter-gatherers to expand into large, secure, and complex social structures. According to the archaeologists, the antihunger technology of grain storage (be it up in a tree or buried underground) dates back eleven thousand years, and almost every civilization since has left ruins of its silos.

The Chinese founded their national grain reserve in 54 BCE, when Keng Shou-ch'ang, the assistant grand minister of agriculture, proposed that all of the provinces along the boundary of the empire create stores of rice for the inevitable day of catastrophe. The Chinese grain reserve has been in place ever since, its volume and dimension a state secret.

Cargill, the largest private company in the world, began its business in 1865 with a grain silo. Today it is believed that Cargill stores more grain than any other company on Earth. But no one knows for sure, because Cargill executives keep the amount of grain they store a secret.

I had never considered a silo as much more than a quaint silhouette on a country road—certainly not a mainstay of human civilization, economy, and politics—but now that I was standing in front of one, I asked Lewis if I could climb inside and take a look. "Sure," he said. "Don't break your leg."

Only yesterday, he and his staff had filled one of his bins with 150 tons of freshly cut hard white winter wheat, harvested somewhere on the unhedged boundaries of the Lewis family farm. Wheat, I learned, comes in many forms and varieties. There is red wheat and white wheat; durum, emmer, and spelt; soft wheat and hard wheat; winter wheat and spring wheat. If Lewis had left Wall Street to make a grain silo his new bank of choice, interest was accruing, for the price of wheat on the Chicago Mercantile Exchange was going up.

Lewis's grain storage possessed the sharp angles, slow curves, and minimalist lines of the architecture of Ludwig Mies van der Rohe. I made my way up the metal rungs that snaked along the steel sides, figured out how to flip open the hatch on top, and slowly maneuvered myself onto the ladder that sank straight down inside the vault.

A pile of grayish raw wheat berries rose from the floor, shifting and shushing as thirty-foot mechanized augers aerated the stock. I had heard that old-time traders from Kansas City and Minneapolis could estimate the price of a bushel by the chew of a kernel: the gummier, the more glutinous; the more glutinous, the more protein content; the more protein content, the more expensive. So when I reached the bottom of the ladder I swept my hand through the warm, dry grains and tossed a few into my mouth. They were gummy, but I couldn't put a price on it.

That evening, Lewis invited his farm interns to an end-of-summer barbecue. After a long day of inseminating cows, lugging granite, and plowing fields, the agriculture majors from Clemson, Purdue, and Minnesota convened on Lewis's large lawn to polish off hamburgers, hot dogs, and grilled chicken.

As dinner came to an end, Lewis stood at the head of the picnic table and warmed up with a few preliminary declamations on deflation, wasting assets, and the misuse of credit, all of which met with no response. It soon became apparent that the future farmers of America had never heard of the bankruptcy of Bear Stearns, Fannie Mae, Freddie Mac, Lehman Brothers, or AIG; nor did they know about the hundreds of billions spent to rescue Citicorp, Chrysler, and General Motors. Perhaps they had been too busy learning the intricacies of soil science to notice the financial meltdown. Lewis informed the peasants-in-training that the Federal Reserve had just increased its balance sheet by two trillion bucks. The interns helped themselves to more burgers.

"What is money?" Lewis shouted at them. A blueberry cobbler emerged from the kitchen, to great acclaim. *What is money?* His question hung in the manured early evening air of organic farmland, and returned to me during my seven-hour drive back to New York City. Since the origin of anything we might remotely recognize as civilization, food and money have been bound together. But in the beginning, making food come out of the earth had nothing to do with money or markets.

The artificial lake, the farm without runoff, and even the Porsche SUV said the same thing. To Lewis, the cost of a thing did not equal its value. Food possessed value, whereas money was an index. But somehow the index had managed to make people believe it was more important than the food. The system had been reversed. "Call me any time," he said as I got into the car, and I gave him a nod and a smile.

My visit to the Lewis family farm had been a good one. It was hard not to admire Lewis for turning his back on Wall Street, global finance, and the virtual world in order to embrace the rural, the local, and the real. When Professor Yaneer Bar-Yam of the New England Complex Systems Institute had gone to Davos and projected his charts and graphs and pointed his finger, he had pointed to the kind of man Sandy Lewis used to be. But the peasant was not a simple man, and Lewis's enduring obsession with assets, credit, debt, and deflation was more than a vestigial fixation.

Lewis had brought me to the core of the food crisis. Certainly it had to do with peasants. But it also had to do with banks.

7

12

The Price

Despite the predictions Thomas Malthus made in the last decade of the eighteenth century, there was enough food to feed the seven billion people who inhabited Earth in the first decade of the twenty-first century and even enough for the nine or ten or twelve billion people due in 2050. The problem was price. The problem was a billion of the poorest people on Earth bidding against a billion of the richest people for the same corn, soybeans, rice, and wheat.

Hunger is only one piece of a larger puzzle, the puzzle of price. Hunger may be the most horrible symptom of the global food malady, but it is just one symptom. The price of basic farm goods drives world hunger, but it also drives the push for sustainability, the rise of long-distance food from nowhere, the scourge of cheap and unhealthy foods, the single-minded drive to own the smallest molecules of food, the declarations and pledges of the politicians, the global mania for markets, and the profit margins of many of the world's largest corporations.

How did food get its price? That was the question.

I first tried to find an answer by looking at wheat. How does a sixty-pound bushel of wheat get measured in dollars and cents? I figured that anyone interested in food would be interested in the answer. But when I asked around, I learned that the price fluctuations of agricultural commodities did not fascinate my friends, nor did the intricacies of hedging and speculating or the financial history of the Midwest. I discovered a vast indifference to the Chicago Mercantile Exchange's trade in wheat, perhaps because the foodies and food activists knew in their gut that the technicalities of commodity pricing were part and parcel of metafood. Food futures had little to do with the real thing, my friends rightly reasoned, and they were interested in food, not derivatives. And I still did not understand enough about global wheat to convince anyone that metabread had become the power behind the throne.

As for my friends who were bankers and traders—they were not particularly interested in exploring how their professions might be responsible for starving a billion people. So I did not pursue the matter with them.

There was a chasm between the world of finance and the world of food, a rift that should not have existed. Food and money had been partners for thousands of years, and now they had become one and the same, but only in a way that experts in commodity markets could understand. I knew I was on to something, but I could hardly say what it was. So I called Sandy Lewis again.

As usual, he was in a bad mood. He was furious at the latest move of the Federal Reserve, or perhaps it was the latest article in the business section of the *New York Times* or the latest exchange rate of the U.S. dollar. Lewis was enraged as a general rule, disgusted by the depravity of the bankers, the ignorance of the media, and the unmitigated knavery of the world. But unlike most people, Lewis possessed a rancor and a loathing that were generally informative.

I told him the whole story. I recounted my visits to the corporate headquarters of Tyson Foods and Domino's Pizza, my sojourns to genetic modification labs across the country, and the days and nights I had spent in the press room of Mussolini's white marble palace in Rome. I told him about the question I had asked Bill Gates at U.N. headquarters in New York. Lewis said nothing. I told him that all my questions had brought me to one question: How did food get its price? Still he said nothing.

"How do people make money?" he finally asked.

I told him I did not know.

"Buy at ten and sell at twelve," he said. "But what makes it go from ten to twelve?"

Now it was my turn to say nothing.

"You have to understand markets," he told me. "There are sets of things that go up and down together."

That brought Lewis back to dollars. As the Federal Reserve prints trillions of dollars, he explained, the value of each individual dollar falls. As the value of the U.S. currency falls, the prices of international commodities (which are priced in U.S.

dollars) go up—and investments in crude oil, gold, and palladium look better and better. The best tactic of all would be to get your hands on as much fresh water and good farmland as possible, said Lewis. Barring that, how about a stake in commodities across the board, from coffee and cocoa to corn and milk and wheat?

How could investors take such positions? "Ah," Lewis murmured. "Ma Goldman." He meant Goldman Sachs, the investment bank founded in Manhattan's Financial District in 1869—just around the time the modern futures markets in wheat began to boom. Over the years, Goldman had grown to become one of the largest financial institutions in the world, but its corporate headquarters remained in Lower Manhattan in a sparkling new skyscraper that rose next to the World Trade Center, just a few blocks from where I lived.

Lewis had made a study of Ma Goldman. In 1981, he told me, the bank had purchased a commodities trading firm called J. Aron and Company, and along with the acquisition had come a host of commodity traders, among them Goldman's future CEO, Lloyd Blankfein. Lewis explained that since the acquisition of J. Aron, commodity trading had become the model for Goldman's business. And he explained that within the world of investment banks, traders possess a distinct personality type and a worldview that can be summed up as follows: anything can be traded.

"Lehman Brothers used to trade cotton," Lewis told me. "Loeb Rhodes traded rubber in what was a French colony known as Vietnam. What you have to realize is there isn't anything you think of today that is not a commodity. Seaweed. Rock. Drainage. Water."

"Let's step back," I said, "and—"

"Imagine the entire world is a checkerboard," Lewis interrupted. "Every single value is a spot on the board. Furniture
has a spot. Corneal transplants have a spot. Things go up and
down. It is giant, it is huge—magnificent in size! And things
go up and down all the time."

So I took a look at Ma Goldman and discovered that the history of food took an ominous turn in 1991, when no one was
paying much attention. That was the year Goldman Sachs
surveyed the world's checkerboard of value and decided that
our daily bread would make an excellent investment. It was a
great position for the traders.

Agriculture, rooted in the rhythms of sowing and reaping,
had not captivated the attention of 1980s vintage Wall Street
bankers, whose riches were not emerging from the sale of real
things like wheat or bread—or even real things once removed,
like soy futures or corn futures—but from the manipulation
of ever more ethereal concepts like risk and collateralized
debt. By 1991, nearly everything else that could be recast as a
financial abstraction had already been considered. Food had
been the first derivative, and now it was the last.

And so with accustomed care and precision, Goldman's
analysts and traders went about transforming food into a unified financial concept. They selected eighteen commodifi-
able ingredients and contrived an elixir that included cattle,
coffee, cocoa, corn, hogs, and a couple of varieties of wheat.
They weighted the investment value of each element, blended
and commingled the parts into sums, then reduced what had
been a complicated system of speculation and hedging into

a mathematical formula that could be expressed as a single manifestation, to be known henceforth as the Goldman Sachs Commodity Index (GSCI). Then they began to offer shares.

Not everyone was interested. One hedge fund manager recalled an intimate dinner on Manhattan's Upper East Side many years ago with representatives from the GSCI. "They were probably hoping I would want to use the index myself," he told me, "but I thought it was a misnomer to look at all commodity prices as some sort of unified entity. What drives gold is totally different from what drives base metals and from what drives soy and corn. Basically, the whole thing is a sham."

Such qualms were not the norm.

As might be expected, Goldman's new index product flourished. The prices of cattle, coffee, cocoa, corn, and wheat began to rise, slowly at first and then rapidly. As more people sank money into Goldman's food index, other bankers took note and created their own food indexes for their own clients. In 1994, J.P. Morgan established its commodity index fund, and soon thereafter other players entered the scene, including the Chase Physical Commodity Index in 1994 and the AIG Commodity Index in 1998, along with initial offerings from Bear Stearns, Oppenheimer, and Pimco.

Barclays joined the group with eight index funds and raised close to three billion dollars in just over a year. Deutsche Bank introduced a trading tool called Powershares, featuring a fund indexed to corn, wheat, soybeans, and sugar. And if "going long" on food was not aggressive enough, Deutsche also offered shares in a product it called the Agriculture Double Long Exchange-Traded Note.

The banks had perceived a new spot on the checkerboard, which meant new markets, new derivatives, and new ways to make money. Virtual food had become financialized food, and this was the key to the price.

Financialized food was a revelation, but it wasn't an entirely new phenomenon. Back in 1936, Congress had created a commission that curbed excessive speculation in commodity markets and limited large holdings of futures contracts to bona fide hedgers. In other words, banks had to stay out of food. If you wanted to buy a huge stake in grain, you had to be the sort of company that actually used grain, like Quaker Oats, General Mills, or Domino's Pizza.

Years later, the modern-day Commodity Futures Trading Commission (CFTC) continued to set limits on the number of wheat futures contracts that could be held by speculators—those who viewed the commodity markets as nothing but a vast math equation that could yield enormous profits.

In 1991, the position limit for speculators was five thousand wheat futures contracts. But after the invention and widespread imitation of the GSCI, bankers convinced the CFTC that just like General Mills and Quaker Oats, they too were bona fide hedgers. They were trading currency and interest rates, weren't they? They were already hedging their dollars, euros, pounds, riyals, and yuan—and wasn't grain just another currency? Wasn't wheat cash and cash wheat?

Eventually, the CFTC caved in to the pressure. It issued something called a position-limit exemption to six commodity index traders, and within a decade those index funds would be permitted to hold as many as 130,000 wheat futures contracts at a time. All of a sudden, bankers could take as large a position in grains as they liked—an opportunity that since the

Great Depression had been available only to those who actually had something to do with the production of food.

"We have not seen U.S. agriculture rely this much on the market for almost seventy years" was how Joseph Dial, the head of the commission, assessed his agency's regulatory handiwork in 1997. "This paradigm shift in the government's farm policy has created a new era for agriculture."

A few weeks after my phone call to Sandy Lewis, I called Steven Rothbart, who had traded commodities for Cargill in the 1980s. I told him I was interested in finding out how a bushel of wheat got its price, and I asked him what he knew about the birth of the commodity index funds. Rothbart laughed. "Commodities had died," he told me. "We sat there every day, and the market wouldn't move. People left. They couldn't make a living anymore."

Brokers and bankers make their money off the ups and downs of the market, movement that is generally known as *volatility*. The direction of the movement doesn't matter all that much, as long as the market moves. But if the market isn't moving, well, clearly some innovation is in order. And so, in the midst of a dead-still market, Goldman Sachs sought a fix. On the political level, the bankers lobbied the CFTC to deregulate commodity markets, an effort that met with success in the last years of the twentieth century.

At the same time, the bankers envisioned an entirely new commodities investor: one who had no taste for the complexities of corn, soy, or wheat; no interest in weather and weevils; and no desire for getting into and out of the short and long positions of the futures market's traditional participants. The new commodity investor envisioned by Goldman wanted nothing more than to park a great deal of money somewhere, then sit back and watch that pile grow, as though food were stocks or bonds.

The intent of the GSCI and other commodity index funds was to transform an investment in corn, soy, and wheat into something that looked a great deal like an investment in General Electric or Microsoft. And once an investment in the commodity market had been made to appear more like an investment in the stock market, bankers could expect huge new influxes of ready cash from people who had never before invested in corn, soy, or wheat—like the people who ran state pension funds, sovereign wealth funds, and private hedge funds.

The structure of the GSCI did not conform to the centuries-old patterns of the futures market, the buying and selling patterns of traditional hedgers and speculators, the patterns based on the ancient cycles of planting, harvesting, and processing of grain, patterns created to stabilize the price of food. In his testimony to the U.S. Senate Committee on Energy and Natural Resources in September 2008, Gary Cohn, Goldman's president, explained the new set of ideas and concepts that lay behind the birth of the GSCI, ideas which had nothing to do with food.

"There was no natural long in the market," Cohn told the Senate committee. "The consumers are so fragmented that they don't amalgamate to a big enough position. So we actually, as a firm, came up with the idea in the early 1990s to create a long-only, static investor in the commodity markets."

What Cohn meant can be summed up as follows: Markets were only as good as the profits that could be extracted from them. And in the case of the stable commodities futures markets, the time had come for a nudge in the right direction, toward the ever profitable volatility of boom and bust. For more than a century, traditional buying and selling on the Chicago Exchange, the Kansas City Board of Trade, and other assorted commodity clearinghouses across the country had helped to keep the price of grain on an even keel. This century of stable food prices had, not coincidentally, witnessed the nation's greatest development and power.

But traditional buying and selling did not satisfy the new generation of banker-traders. As a result, the tactics of the GSCI had little in common with the long-standing structures of the futures market. The GSCI was not made for farmers and millers to lock in price guarantees so they could plan for the future and remove some risk from an inherently risky business. The GSCI was not even made for market speculators who buy low, sell high, and cancel out their positions before any wheat passes through their hands.

In fact, the GSCI had been designed in opposition to the fundamental patterns of all markets. The index fund was "long-only," which meant that it had been built to amass promises to buy commodities, and *only buy*. The GSCI did not include a mechanism to sell, or "short," any of the commodities on the index. Long-only was the index trader's brilliant insight—even if the buy-and-only-buy structure of the GSCI accelerated grain's natural propensities toward scarcity and glut, the very elements the futures markets had been designed to steady.

This is how long-only worked: The managers of the GSCI would acquire and hold numerous long positions—promises to buy precious metals, oil, agriculture, and livestock at a future date. But unlike the farmer, the miller, or the baker, the banker would not protect his position on the futures market with the actual sale or purchase of real wheat—like a bona fide hedger—nor would he cover his long position by eventually selling short and making a profit in the grand old fashion of commodities speculators. In fact, the structure of commodity index funds ran counter to our normal understanding of economic theory, for the GSCI demanded that index-fund managers not buy low and sell high, but buy and *keep buying at any price*.

No matter what heights wheat, oil, or gold futures might attain, whenever contracts became due on the futures markets, the GSCI managers would transfer their long positions into the next long futures contract, which would expire a few months later; then when that contract was about to expire, they would repeat the "roll" into the next futures contract down the line—thus accumulating an everlasting, ever growing demand for future wheat. This was the "natural long" that Cohn had mentioned to the U.S. Senate, and it was not at all natural. "They had to breathe life into this market," said Rothbart, the ex-Cargill trader. "But you've got to be out of your freaking mind to be long-only. Commodities are the riskiest things in the world."

Investing in commodities had now become riskier than ever before. But Goldman had figured out its own way to offset the hazards of commodities trading—if not for its clients, then at least for itself. The strategy, which became standard practice for most index funds, relied on a banking technique called *replication*. This meant that for every dollar a client invested in the index fund, Goldman would buy a dollar's worth of the underlying commodities futures (minus management fees, of course). But in order to hold commodities futures, the bankers only had to make a good-faith deposit of about 5 percent of the total investment to their margin account at the exchange; this meant they could stash the other 95 percent of their investors' money in a pool of U.S. Treasury bills, or some other equally innocuous financial cranny, which they could subsequently leverage into ever greater amounts of capital to utilize for their own ends, whatever they might be.

If the price of wheat went up, Goldman made money. And if the price of wheat fell, Goldman still made money—not only from management fees but also from the profits the bank received by putting 95 percent of the clients' money into the hands of genius-boy day traders who would invest in whatever happened to be the most lucrative trading program of the minute. Goldman and its imitators even made money from the roll into each new long contract, every instance of which required the clients to pay a new set of transaction costs. And since the deflationary impact of selling a position simply wasn't part of the GSCI, professional grain traders could make a killing as each grain contract neared its expiration date.

"That's the way the Goldmans and Morgans make their money," a New York–based hedge fund manager told me. "At first the roll was done mechanically—then they noticed this would move the markets. They realized they could trade around it. They knew that when the rolls were taking place they could position themselves to make money. They may only be charging what seems to be a small fee, but the opportunity they get to take advantage of the rolls makes them a great business."

Since the grain markets lack transparency, it is hard to know if index fund brokers ever bet against their clients, as was the case with mortgage-backed securities. Then again, an insider stock tip could send a broker to jail, but making a fortune by hitching a ride on a manipulated spike in the price of wheat —a price hike that was simultaneously starving millions of women and children—well, that was perfectly legal.

"In equity land, we have a slew of laws saying if you act on insider information you go to jail," a fund manager explained to me. "But there's no such thing on currency markets and commodity markets. There's no such thing as insider information."

That insight took a while to sink in. In commodity markets, insider trading is no crime. No surprise, then, that commodity brokers employed by the banks that had created the commodity index funds in the first place found that the once moribund grain market was now producing boatloads of cash. A commodity trader named Emil van Essen told *Business-Week* in 2010, "I make a living off the dumb money." Profitability had returned to the grain markets, even if the price of the world's food had begun to rise, and no one could say why.

The bankers had figured out how to extract money from the grain and livestock commodity exchanges without taking on any of the risks they themselves had introduced to the global market. Unlike the wheat producers, processors, millers, and bakers and even Goldman's own customers, Goldman had no vested interest in a stable commodities market, in those who invested in their funds, or in food itself. As one index trader told me, "Commodity funds have historically made money— and kept most of it for themselves."

Dozens of banks flocked into long-only commodity index funds, making easy money through their rolls and safeguarding themselves from loss and risk through replication. But there was even more money to be made if the banks could somehow convince everyone else that a product designed to protect the banks—and only the banks—was in fact also safe for every investor. At that point, academic studies began to appear.

Just a few months after the bursting of the dot-com bubble, the first influential intellectual treatise on commodity index funds ran in the summer 2000 issue of the *Journal of Alternative Investments*. Robert Greer, a vice president of the Global Commodities Group at what was then the Chase Manhattan Bank, advocated an index of commodities as its own distinct asset class, suitable for institutional investors. Traditionally, commodity markets had been too complicated and risky for institutional investors, but the single line of the index fund graph made the intricacies of light sweet crude oil and Kansas City winter wheat easy to grasp, even for the nonspecialists who sat on the boards of state pension funds. Greer's study burnished the credentials of this new derivative, the commodity index fund, and helped assuage the traditional fears of the futures markets.

Five years after Greer's article appeared, Gary Gorton, of the University of Pennsylvania, and K. Geert Rouwenhorst, of the Yale University School of Management, published a working paper called *Facts and Fantasies about Commodities Futures*. In forty graph-and-equation-filled pages, the authors demonstrated that between 1959 and 2004, a hypothetical investment in a broad range of commodities—such as a commodity index fund—would have been no more risky than an investment in a broad range of stocks. What's more, Gorton and Rouwenhorst asserted that commodities exhibited a negative correlation with equities and a positive correlation with inflation. Translation: Not only was a commodity index fund a legitimate spot to allocate assets, but food was always a good investment—and even better in bad times.

As the monk Joshua the Stylite came to understand in 499, the worse things got, the higher the cost of chickpeas and lentils. When the locusts descend, why not invest?

Money managers could hardly wait to spread the news. "Since this discovery," reported the *Financial Times* of London, investors had become attracted to commodities "in the hope that returns will differ from equities and bonds and be strong in case of inflation."

"Commodities can be considered a separate strategic asset class," declared *Global Pensions*, a magazine that characterizes itself as "intelligence for the sophisticated scheme investor." Another study noted that commodity index funds offered "an inherent or natural return that is not conditioned on skill."

Numerous articles began to pop up in other publications, such as the *Journal of Finance*, the *Journal of Portfolio Management*, the *Journal of Derivatives*, and the *Derivatives Quarterly*, all arguing that an investment in an index of commodities would enhance portfolios. By the middle of 2008, the databases that record such things listed more than eight hundred "managed futures" funds.

A shimmering new casino of food derivatives had opened its doors, and just at the opportune moment. In the dawning century of climate change, scarcity, and political and economic upheaval, as currencies faltered and debts became due, an investment in commodities was sure to succeed. During the darkest of times, through droughts and floods, fires and freezes, an investment in commodities would thrive. Even in the event of "cartel intervention" (I imagined this meant some monstrous multinational trying to corner the market), commodity prices only increased. And when things get really bad—think war and hyperinflation—nothing can beat commodities.

A few years after Gorton and Rouwenhorst's paper appeared, and almost as though to prove everybody's point, financial disaster plowed through the mortgage, credit, and real estate markets, and just as the index-fund scholars had predicted, those who had invested in commodities prospered. Institutional investors, money manager Michael Masters noted on his blog, "decided en masse to embrace commodities futures as an investable asset class." At which point the long-awaited legion of new investors rushed into commodity index funds, and the food bubble began.

The new crowd of commodity investors were neither buyers nor sellers of corn, wheat, or soy. Nor were they versed in the complexities of harvest and milling. Nor were they expert speculators—trend-obsessed grain heads focused on the technicalities of price fluctuation. "You had people who had no clue what commodities were all about suddenly buying commodities," one analyst from the U.S. Department of Agriculture told me.

No matter. In the first fifty-five days of 2008, the new food-money investors poured $55 billion into commodity exchanges, and by July, $318 billion was roiling what had previously been a backwater. "Although Commodity Trading Advisors are a subset of the hedge funds universe, they control a significant amount of assets," noted a 2008 paper from the Yale International Center for Finance that carried the sobering title "Fooling Some of the People All of the Time."

In the first decade of this century, hundreds of billions of new dollars poured into food derivatives and changed the market forever. Food had become just another avenue of asset allocation, and the more the price of food rose, the better for the investor—and the more money poured into the grain markets. If no one contemplated the effects that this accumulation of long-only futures would have on the grain markets, perhaps it was because no one had ever seen such a massive pile of long-only grain futures.

From one perspective, a complicated chain of cause and effect had sparked the food bubble. But there were those who understood what was happening to the wheat markets in simpler terms. "I don't have to pay anybody for anything, basically," one long-only indexer told me. "That's the beauty of it."

13

Hard Red Spring

North America, the Saudi Arabia of cereal, sends nearly half of the wheat it produces overseas, and since 1881 an obscure syndicate known as the Minneapolis Grain Exchange (MGEX) has remained the supreme price setter for the continent's most widely exported wheat, a high-protein variety called hard red spring. North American hard red spring supplies the bakeries of the Middle East, and its price informs the cost of virtually every loaf of bread on Earth. Other kinds of wheat make cake and cookies, but only hard red spring makes bread.

On the MGEX, the global food crisis could be gauged by the ever quickening uptick of fifths of a cent. Hard red spring had long traded between three and six dollars per sixty-pound bushel, but from 2005 to 2008 Minneapolis wheat broke record after record as its price doubled, then doubled again.

The news media hardly covered the spike. Who cared about hard red spring wheat? Who had ever heard of it? What could be more boring than agricultural markets? And as for all those hungry people, weren't there always hungry people? Except for a few nonprofits and scattered activists, no one noted the looming crisis.

Then, in late February 2008, daily trading in hard red spring wheat set records for both single-day gains and single-day declines, and everyone in the business perceived that a new force had entered the market. "Anyone who tells you they've seen something like this is a liar," said a trader from South Dakota. And then, on February 25, as the Dow Jones Industrial Average slunk to the bottom of an eighteen-month low, the price of hard red spring surged 29 percent and closed at a record twenty-four dollars per bushel, roughly quadruple the highest number it had ever reached.

To put this price in perspective, imagine the Dow shooting up twelve thousand points in one day to top out at forty-eight thousand. "Volatility is out of control," declared Joe Victor, a grain analyst and the vice president of Allendale, one of the largest commodity research firms, in McHenry, Illinois. As the price of wheat shot up and down, the Commodity Futures Trading Commission (CFTC) kept watch from its offices in Chicago, Kansas City, New York City, and Washington, D.C. The agency possesses emergency powers to *maintain or restore orderly trading*, a power it did not wield. In fact, at the height of hard red spring's historic run, the CFTC did quite the opposite: it agreed to remove price limits on hard red spring futures.

The price of wheat reverberates throughout the global food chain. Of course, it is rational to invest in a commodity when its price rises, even if wheat costs push up corn costs and corn costs push up feed prices. Chickens eat chicken feed made from that corn, so the price of a dozen organic eggs hits $6.39. "All indications are that soaring feed costs are going to force livestock and poultry producers to raise prices," said Joel Brandenberger, the president of the National Turkey Federation.

Bill Roenigk, the chief economist of the National Chicken Council, took the long view, predicting that "food inflation is poised to begin and continue for many, many months." All of which impelled Senator Charles Grassley of Iowa to wax rabid and liken the U.S. grocery lobby to the Nazi Party. "They have to have an excuse for increasing the price of their food," said Grassley. "It's another Adolf Hitler lie." But the U.S. grocery lobby was not to blame.

It is rational to invest in a commodity when its price rises, even if the effects of the investment spark conflagrations of irrationality. For the boom in global grain, edible oils, and livestock had created a vicious cycle. The more the price of food commodities increased, the more money poured into the sector and the higher the prices rose. And so, from 2003 to 2008, the volume of commodity index fund speculation increased by 1,900 percent.

"What we are experiencing is a demand shock coming from a new category of participant in the commodities futures markets," hedge fund manager Michael Masters testified to

Congress on May 20, 2008. "It's unprecedented how much investment capital we've seen in commodity markets," said Kendell Keith, the president of the National Grain and Feed Association. "There's no question there's been speculation."

As $200 billion new dollars plunked into commodities, 250 million new people descended into poverty. From 2005 to 2008 the worldwide price of food rose 80 percent, and no one was surprised when the *Economist* announced that the real price of food had reached its highest level since 1845, the year the magazine first calculated the number.

Some grain transnationals had anticipated the effects of the commodity index funds. Cargill attributed its 86 percent jump in annual profits to commodity trading, and ConAgra sold its trading arm to a private equity firm for $2.8 billion. But while Cargill and ConAgra took profits, General Mills reported a $111 million loss on its hedges. "The volatility can wreak havoc on profits," reported *Business Week*.

Meanwhile, Italians found the price of pasta to be higher than ever, Russians had to pay more for cabbage, and Korean kimchi went through the roof. American chicken, milk, and egg prices all advanced in double digits. The scenario played out just as Harvard economist Amartya Sen had predicted: childhood hunger in the United States increased by one half. Demand for food stamps soared. "The poor who struggled to feed themselves when prices were low were virtually shut out of the market as prices quadrupled," wrote University of Tennessee agricultural analyst Daryll Ray.

Nothing had changed about the wheat, but something had changed about the wheat market. Since Goldman Sachs's innovation, hundreds of billions of new dollars had overwhelmed the actual supply and actual demand for it, and rumors began to circulate that someone somewhere had cornered the market.

In all of recorded history, only one person had ever cornered the grain market, and that was the biblical patriarch Joseph. An ex-slave and an ex-con, Joseph was a speculator in the most traditional sense of the word: he was able to see what others could not. When Joseph emerged from prison darkness, he saw through the mists of Pharaoh's strange dreams, in which seven fat cattle were devoured by seven emaciated cattle and seven fat ears of corn were consumed by seven decayed ears of corn. Joseph saw that Pharaoh's dreams were grain futures, a prediction of seven years of plenty followed by seven years of famine.

So Joseph went long on wheat. He amassed the greatest grain silos in ancient history, and when seven years of plenty were followed by seven years of drought, the price of grain doubled and doubled again and Joseph brought the nations of the earth to their knees—and became a very, very rich man.

Ever since Joseph, robber barons, gold bugs, and financiers of every stripe have dreamed of controlling all of something everybody needed or desired, then holding back the supply as demand drove up prices. But oddly enough, there was plenty of real wheat in 2008, and U.S. farmers were delivering it as fast as they always had, if not even a bit faster. It was as though the price itself had begun to generate its own demand: the more hard red spring wheat cost, the more investors wanted to pay for it.

Even the mainstream media began to note the novelty. "Odd Crop Prices Defy Economics," read a headline in the *New York Times* on March 28, 2008.

"It's absolutely mind-boggling," a grain trader told the *Wall Street Journal*.

"You don't ever want to trade wheat again," another told the *Chicago Tribune*.

"We have never seen anything like this before," Jeff Voge, the chairman of the Kansas City Board of Trade, told the *Washington Post*. "This isn't just any commodity. It is food, and people need to eat."

So crashed the dreams of the Food and Agriculture Organization of the United Nations, the dreams of the World Bank, the dreams of the International Fund for Agricultural Development, and the dreams of the World Food Program—the dreams of global food secured by global markets. That old hobgoblin, nationalism, had reappeared.

"To cope with high prices, countries have been rationing supplies by leveling tariffs or taxes on grain exports," reported the *Wall Street Journal* on February 28, 2008. Fifteen countries capped or halted their wheat exports. Export restrictions in Kazakhstan, Russia, Ukraine, and Argentina closed off a third of the global market.

The results were drastic. As Jordan scoured world markets for wheat, Syria canceled export contracts. Foreign buyers from South Korea, Taiwan, Mexico, Nigeria, and Venezuela pumped up the market just as Japan was bidding for 85,000 tons of U.S. spring wheat. In February 2008, Chicago traders woke up to learn that Iraq had purchased more than 550,000 tons of hard red winter wheat overnight. And the price of food shot up even more.

"We can see now that the world has largely failed in its attempt to create an integrated food market," said Richard Feltes, the senior vice president of MF Global, the futures brokerage house that would crash and burn only three years later. "If you don't feed your country, it's civil war," said NatWest Securities analyst David C. Nelson. The revolutions would come later.

What was the nature of the grain that had exploded in price and transformed the price of the world's bread?

Hard red spring wheat was a supergrain, a spiritual descendant of the new wheats that emigrated to the United States more than a century ago, just about the time the great grain merchants of the Midwest created the modern commodity markets, and just around the time a peddler named Marcus Goldman hung out a shingle on Pine Street in downtown Manhattan and started dealing IOUs. It was just around this time—1866, to be precise—that a Kansas farm boy named Mark Alfred Carleton was born.

Carleton may have been the first American to be entirely obsessed by wheat. His particular desire was to discover a variety that would ripen despite extreme weather conditions—wheat that was not only frost resistant but ice-storm resistant. Carleton wanted wheat that would not blow out of the parched Kansas ground when blasts of arid wind careened down from the Rocky Mountains. He wanted drought resistance and disease resistance, too.

Much like the food prospectors and scientists I had met at Ohio State, UC-Davis, and the USDA's Agricultural Research Station in Corvallis, Mark Carleton criss-crossed the United States. He found Russian Mennonites on the Great Plains raising winter wheats with kernels so unyielding and impervious they broke the stones of commercial mills. And while other wheats had failed across the Great Plains, these Russian farmers enjoyed good harvests. At which point Carleton became fixated on Russia. He learned the language, studied the geographical similarities of the semiarid steppes with the semiarid plains, and became convinced that the answer to American hunger was Siberian wheat.

In 1898 the U.S. secretary of agriculture granted Carleton permission to become an international food prospector and tour the Russian steppes, so he sailed to England, made his way through the capitals of France, Belgium, Germany, Denmark, Sweden, Austria, Hungary, and Romania, and finally entered Russia at Odessa, near the Black Sea, the heart of wheat country. Carleton was on an epic journey, as fabulous as the ancient trek of Pharaoh Hatshepsut to the Land of Punt to fetch frankincense and myrrh.

Carleton traveled from the Ukraine south to Baku (now the capital of Azerbaijan), collecting grains of Kharkov wheat from the Kirghiz Steppes. In Kubanka, he collected durum, which he thought would do well across the thousand-mile stretch from Texas to Colorado. Then it was on to the Volga River and more kinds of wheat, oats, barley, millet, and emmer. When he returned to the United States, Carleton brought with him twenty-three new cereals.

Then the hard part began. Carleton had to test his Russian varieties against an international all-star team of wheats: the Onigara from Japan, the Haffkani from Turkey, the Kaiser from Germany, the Prolifero from Italy, and Australia's Rattling Jack. When Carleton finally proved what he had long suspected, he vowed to spread his Russian wheat from Kansas to Nebraska, Oklahoma, and Montana. By 1914, half of the U.S. annual yield of winter wheat was Carleton's variety, more than eighty million bushels. For none of the Midwest's wheat is native. It was a Muslim wheat from Siberia that brought security to the United States.

On a plane to Minneapolis I read a startling prediction. "It may be hard to imagine commodity prices advancing another 460 percent above their mid-2008 price peaks," hedge fund manager John Hummel wrote in a letter to clients of AIS Capital Management. "But the fundamentals argue strongly [that] these sectors have significant upside potential." Like most commodity men, Hummel welcomed the apocalypse, which presents "a significant investment opportunity." I made a quick calculation: 460 percent above 2008 peaks meant ground beef at twenty dollars a pound.

From my hotel, I put in a call to Michael Ricks, the chairman of the Minneapolis Grain Exchange. In addition to his responsibilities at MGEX, Ricks was Cargill's merchandising manager in charge of North America, and a member of the Technology Advisory Committee of the CFTC. Such a plethora of possible conflicts of interest is not atypical in the commodities business.

Could food prices rise even higher? I asked.

"Absolutely," said Ricks. "We're in a volatile world."

Later that afternoon I talked to a number of other higher-ups at MGEX, including Layne Carlson, the corporate secretary and treasurer. I asked Carlson the same question I had asked Ricks: Could the price of wheat rise even higher?

"Yes," said Carlson, who then told me the two principles that govern the movement of grain markets: "fear and greed."

But wasn't it part of a grain exchange's responsibility to ensure a stable valuation of our daily bread?

"I view what we're working with as widgets," said Todd Posthuma, MGEX's associate director of market operations and information technology, the man who was at that time responsible for clearing a hundred million dollars worth of trades every day. "I think being an employee at an exchange is different from adding value to the food system."

The next morning I walked through the snow to the Minneapolis Grain Exchange, the name of which conjures images of an immense concrete silo towering over a prairie. But the MGEX is, in fact, a rather severe neoclassical steel-frame building that shares the downtown corner of Fourth Street and Fourth Avenue with City Hall, the courthouse, and the jail. I walked through the vestibule of granite and Italian marble, past renderings of wheat molded into the terra-cotta cartouches, and as I waited for the wheat-embossed elevator I tried not to gawk at the gold-plated mail chute.

For more than a century, the trading floor of MGEX had been the place where hard red spring wheat acquired a price, but as I stepped out of the elevator, the opening bell tolled and echoed across a vast, silent, and chilly chamber. The place was abandoned, the phones ripped out of the walls, the octagonal grain pits littered with snakes of tangled wire.

I wandered across the wooden planks of the old pits, scarred by the boots of countless grain traders, and peered into the dark and narrow recesses of the phone booths where the brokers and traders had scribbled their orders. Beyond the booths loomed the massive cash-grain tables, illuminated by long shafts of sunlight. In the old days, when brokers and traders looked into one another's faces, they liked to examine the grain before they bought it.

The U.S. derivatives markets were born in these octagonal trading pits, as in the octagonal pits of Chicago, Kansas City, and New Orleans. Here, the first modern hedgers and speculators arbitraged wheat from Sheboygan, Mackinac, and Duluth and rode the waves of a titanic market that exported the staff of life from West to East, from the New World to the Old.

Above the grain pits, an electronic board began to populate with green, red, and yellow numbers that told the price of barley, canola, cattle, coffee, copper, cotton, gold, hogs, lumber, milk, oats, oil, platinum, rice, and silver. Beneath them shimmered the indexes: the Dow and Standard & Poor's 500 and, at the very bottom, the Goldman Sachs Commodity Index, which S&P had bought in 2007 for an undisclosed amount. Even the video technology was quaint, a relic from the late 1970s, when trade with the Soviet Union was the final frontier, long before the moment early in the twenty-first century when the CEO of MGEX, Mark Bagan, decided that the future of wheat was not on a table in Minneapolis but within the infinitude of the Internet.

Electronic wheat could be bought and sold from any screen, anywhere on Earth, and Bagan had suspected that more people than ever would trade the hard red spring contract once wheat became digital. And he was right.

But as a courtesy to the grain brokers who for decades had spent their days hedging and speculating in the grain pits, MGEX had furnished a gray-carpeted room a few stories above the old trading floor. Here a few dozen beige cubicles were available to rent. Some of the cubicles faced the

Mississippi River and offered views of the ruins of the old Gold Medal Flour factory. Others faced a parking lot.

I had expected shouting, panic, confusion, and chaos, but no more than half of the cubicles were occupied, and the room was silent. One of the grain traders was reading his e-mail, another checking ESPN for the weekend sports scores, another playing solitaire, another shopping on eBay for antique Japanese vases.

"We're trading wheat, but it's wheat we're never going to see," Austin Damiani, a twenty-eight-year-old wheat broker, told me later that afternoon. "It's a cerebral experience."

That day's action consisted of a gray-haired man padding from cubicle to cubicle, greeting colleagues while sucking hard candy. The veteran eventually ambled off to a corner where a battered cash-grain table had been moved up from the old trading floor. A dozen aluminum pans sat on the table, each holding a different sample of grain. The old man brought a pan to his face and took a deep breath. Then he held a single grain in his palm, turned it over, and found the crease. "The crease will tell you the variety," he told me. "That's a lost art."

His name was Mike Mullin, he had been trading wheat for fifty years, and he was the first Minneapolis wheat trader I had seen touch a grain of the stuff. Back in the day, buyers and sellers might have spent hours insulting, cajoling, bullying, and pleading with one another across this table—anything to get the right price for hard red spring—but Mullin was not buying real wheat today, nor was anybody here selling it.

Above us, three monitors flickered prices from the primary U.S. grain exchanges: Chicago, Kansas City, and Minneapolis. Such geographic specificities struck me as archaic, but there remain essential differences among these wheat markets, vestiges of old-fashioned concerns such as latitude and proximity to the Erie Canal.

Mullin stared at the screens and asked me what I knew about wheat futures, and I told him that whereas Minneapolis traded the contract in hard red spring, Kansas City traded in hard red winter and Chicago in soft red winter—both of which have a lower protein content than Minneapolis wheat, are less expensive, and are more likely to be incorporated into a brownie mix than into a baguette. High protein content makes Minneapolis wheat elite, I told Mullin.

He nodded his head, and we stood in silence and watched the desultory movement of corn and soy, soft red winter and hard red spring. It was a slow trading day even if agricultural commodities, as Mullin told me, were overpriced 10 percent across the board. Mullin figured he knew the real worth of a bushel and had bet the price would soon head south. "Am I short?" he asked. "Yes I am."

I asked him what he knew about the commodity indexes, like the one Goldman Sachs had created in 1991. "It's a brainless entity," Mullin said. His eyes did not move from the screen. "You look at a chart. You hit a number. You buy."

14

The Bubble Business

The year 2008 witnessed the greatest wheat crop in human history. That year also witnessed the greatest number of starving people in human history. And 2008 witnessed a historic run on the price of hard red spring wheat.

While those who follow the grain markets were scratching their heads over the food bubble, still trying to figure out what had happened to the price of global wheat, Mark Bagan, the CEO of the Minneapolis Grain Exchange (MGEX), invited me to his office for a talk. A self-proclaimed "grain brat," Bagan grew up among bales, combines, and concrete silos all across the United States before attending Minnesota

State University to play football. As I settled into his over-sized couch, admired his neatly tailored pin-striped suit, and listened to his soft voice, it occurred to me that if the grain markets were a casino, Bagan was the biggest bookie. Without him, there could be no bets on hard red spring. "From our perspective, we're price neutral, value neutral," he said.

Above Bagan's desk hung a jagged chart of hard red spring futures, mapping every peak and valley from 1973 to 2006. The highs on Bagan's chart reached $7.50. Had 2008's spike to $25 been included, the line would have literally gone through the roof.

But it occurred to me that Bagan was less interested in the price of wheat than in the volume of wheat contracts traded on his exchange. Since wheat futures are nothing more than promises, the possibilities for growth were, to be precise, infinite. The more people traded the hard red spring contract, the more the price moved, the better for MGEX.

I asked Bagan if he thought the price of wheat would rise again. Would there be another food bubble? "The flow of money into commodities has changed significantly in the last decade," he explained. "Wheat, corn, soft commodities—I don't see these dollars going away. It already has happened," he said. "It's inevitable."

Like Joseph in Egypt, Mark Bagan beheld the future. There was a new flow of money, a new square rising on the checkerboard of global value.

I asked Bagan about the growth of commodity index funds and whether this new breed of derivative had transformed traditional grain markets into something wholly speculative, artificial, and virtual. Why did anyone except bankers need this new index of imaginary wheat?

"There are plenty of markets out there that have yet to be thought of and will be very successful," Bagan said, then he digressed into the intricacies of running a commodities exchange. "With our old system, we could clear forty-eight products. Now we can have more than fifty thousand products traded. It's a big number, building derivatives on top of derivatives, but we've got to be prepared for that. The financial world is evolving so quickly, there will always be a need for new risk-management products."

I took this to mean that Bagan had big plans for MGEX. But the CEO had not answered my question about the effect of the commodity index funds. So I asked again, as directly as I could: What did he make of the fact that unprecedented levels of speculation had emerged from a new universe of investors and caused a global run on the price of hard red spring wheat?

Bagan slowly shook his head, as though he were an elementary school teacher trying to explain a basic concept—subtraction? ice?—to a particularly dense child. The Goldman Sachs Commodity Index (GSCI) did not include a single hard red spring future, he told me. Minneapolis wheat may have set records in 2008 and led global food prices into the stratosphere and hundreds of millions into misery, but neither the boom nor the misery had anything to do with a new breed of investors and the index funds.

The GSCI held stakes in the Chicago Mercantile Exchange's soft red winter wheat contract, Bagan told me. And the GSCI held stakes in the Kansas City Board of Trade's hard red winter wheat contract. But there just wasn't enough speculation in MGEX's hard red spring wheat futures contract to satisfy the bankers, so there was no hard red spring from the MGEX in the GSCI.

Bagan smiled. Was there anything else I wanted to know? There was plenty, but Bagan wasn't about to disclose anything more. I still did not know how a bushel of hard red spring got its price, but I had learned that the grain game in Minneapolis was incestuous. In 2009, two companies, Cargill and Archer Daniels Midland, were estimated to control roughly 75 percent of the global cereal trade. Then there was General Mills and the other massive millers, shippers, and warehouses. There were the food processors, the global traders, and John Deere and Monsanto, the manufacturers of seeds, fertilizers, herbicides, and farm machinery. All of these players had invested in seats on MGEX, as had grain brokers from ConAgra, J.P. Morgan Futures, and Prudential Bache Commodities.

As I wandered down the halls of MGEX, I remembered the rumors I had heard at a grain-crisis conference in Washington, D.C., a few months earlier. Between interminable speeches about price ceilings and grain reserves, more than one wheat expert had confided, strictly on background, that at the height of the food bubble, Minneapolis wheat had been cornered. No one could say whether the culprit had been Cargill, the Canadian Wheat Board, or any other party, but the consensus was that as the world had cried for food, someone somewhere had been hoarding wheat.

And it would happen again—inevitably.

The American novelist Frank Norris died in 1902. The next year, Doubleday posthumously published his work *The Pit*, which tells the story of Curtis Jadwin, a "capitalist and speculator" who seeks to corner the market in wheat. "Demand

and supply," wrote Norris, "these were the two great laws the wheat obeyed." He continued:

> Almost blasphemous in his effrontery . . . [Curtis Jadwin] had tampered with these laws, and had roused a Titan. He had laid his puny human grasp upon Creation and the very earth herself, the great mother, feeling the touch of the cobweb that the human insect had spun, had stirred at last in her sleep and sent her omnipotence moving through the grooves of the world, to find and crush the disturber of her appointed courses.

A century after the puny human grasp of Jadwin had failed to close upon wheat, the index funds arose. Like Jadwin, the index traders purchased their wheat futures on the largest grain trading platform in the United States, the Chicago Mercantile Exchange (CME). Founded in 1898 as a clearinghouse for butter and egg futures, the CME had become the world's commodity giant. Recently it paid more than eleven billion dollars to acquire yet another futures market, the New York Mercantile Exchange. Overnight, the CME's traditional list of agricultural commodities grew to include futures contracts in electricity, gasoline, uranium, aluminum, copper, and gold, along with ever more baroque trades in derivatives of interest rates and currencies.

And so I found myself pushing through the frigid blasts of Chicago's LaSalle Street canyon. At the end of the road loomed the CME. If I could figure out how index fund managers on Wall Street trading wheat futures in Chicago had driven up the price of hard red spring in Minneapolis,

I would know why a billion people on the planet could not afford bread.

The man who agreed to escort me to the floor of the CME traded grain for a transnational corporation. He told me several times that his company did not allow him to talk to the press and that if I ever mentioned his name he would lose his job. So I will call him Mr. Silver. I met him before trading hours in the CME's basement cafeteria, where I bought him a breakfast of bacon and eggs and explained why I was interested in grain futures.

I told Silver a little about everything that had led up to that morning, hoping he would eventually be inspired to fill in the blanks. I told him about Domino's Pizza and Tyson Foods, the molecular biologists I had visited in California, and the politicians I had listened to in Rome. I mentioned Sandy Lewis and the great checkerboard of value—a metaphor that did not appear to interest Silver.

So I switched to grain. I described the history of grain hoarding, Joseph in Egypt, Osaka in 1730, the Panic of 1857, and futures contracts for cat pelts, molasses, and onions. I told him about the replication strategy of Goldman Sachs, Gary Gorton and K. Geert Rouwenhorst's 2005 paper on commodity futures facts and fantasies, and the rise and rise of index funds. I told him that at least one analyst had estimated that investments in commodity index funds could easily increase to as much as a trillion dollars, which would result in yet another global food catastrophe, much worse than the one before.

And I told him there was something I still did not understand about the price of a bushel of wheat: the relationship of one commodity grain to another. Kansas City wheat and

Minneapolis wheat and Chicago wheat were all different wheats, traded on different exchanges and with different contracts, but they were all connected. I just didn't get how.

Silver nodded, so I asked him a technical question. Could he explain how index funds that held long-only Chicago wheat futures could have come to dictate the actual price of Minneapolis hard red spring wheat? Silver looked at his scrambled eggs and said nothing.

I mentioned that most of the GSCI was devoted to crude oil, gasoline, heating oil, natural gas, and other energy-based commodities. I knew that wheat was nothing but an indexical afterthought, I told him, accounting for less than 6.5 percent of Goldman's fund. Silver sipped his coffee.

But even 6.5 percent of the GSCI made for a historically unprecedented pile of long wheat futures. Especially when those index funds kept rolling over the contracts they already had, all of them buy orders, only a smattering purchased in Kansas City. None in Minneapolis.

And then the answer occurred to me. It was neither an individual nor a corporation that had cornered the wheat market. The index funds may never have held a single bushel of actual wheat, but they were hoarding staggering quantities of wheat futures—billions of promises to buy, not one of them ever to be fulfilled. The dreaded market corner had emerged not from a shortage in the wheat supply but from a much rarer economic occurrence, a shock to the system inspired by the ceaseless call of food indexes for wheat that did not exist and would never need to exist. Instead of a hidden mastermind committing a dastardly deed, a Joseph in Egypt, or a Curtis Jadwin in turn-of-the-century Chicago, it was what the old Minneapolis wheat trader Mike Mullin had called the "brainless entity."

The investment instrument itself—the index—had taken over and created the effects of a traditional corner. Silver stopped eating his eggs.

I told him that I understood how the index funds' unprecedented accumulation of wheat futures from 2003 to 2008 could create the appearance of a market corner in Chicago. But why had the market for hard red spring in Minneapolis begun to act as though it too had been cornered, when none of the index funds had bought wheat on MGEX? Why had the world's most widely exported wheat doubled in price, then doubled again, causing a billion people—. At this point, Silver interrupted my monologue.

Index-fund buying had pushed up the price of all the Chicago wheat contracts, he said, until the price of imaginary wheat had come to equal the actual price of real wheat—and still Chicago wheat futures surged. The result was contango. I gave Silver a blank look.

Contango, he explained, describes a market in which future prices rise above current prices. Rather than being stable, steady, and backwardated, contango markets tend to be hysterical, overheated, and volatile, with spot prices climbing to catch up with the most outrageously escalated futures prices, which was one of the reasons, between 2006 and 2008, the spot price of Chicago soft red winter soared from three dollars per bushel to eleven.

This was not the futures market John Maynard Keynes had contemplated. Of course, the ever advancing price of wheat and the newfound strength of grain were excellent news for the investors who had flooded commodity index funds with hundreds of billions of dollars. No matter that the mechanism created to stabilize grain prices had been hijacked into a mechanism to inflate grain prices, or that the stubbornly growing discrepancy between futures and spot prices meant that farmers and merchants could no longer use these markets to price crops and manage risks.

Never mind that the long-only indexes had subverted the price-discovery function of the futures market, or that contango in Chicago had disrupted the operations of the nation's grain markets to the extent that the U.S. Senate Committee on Homeland Security and Governmental Affairs had begun an investigation into whether speculation in the wheat markets might pose a threat to interstate commerce. And then there was the question of the millers, the bakers, and the warehousers: those who needed actual wheat to sell, actual bread that might feed actual people.

Silver lowered his voice and told me that as the price of Chicago wheat had bubbled ever upward, commercial buyers had turned elsewhere to purchase the grain they required. They had turned to places like Minneapolis. Hard red spring wheat had been historically more expensive than Chicago's soft red winter wheat, but now it had begun to look like a bargain. So grain brokers bought Minneapolis wheat and left it to the chemists at General Mills or Sara Lee or Papa John's to rejigger their dough recipes for the higher-protein variety.

The brokers purchased hard red spring much earlier in the annual cycle than usual, and they purchased more of it than ever before, as real demand began to chase the ever growing, everlasting long of the commodity index funds. By the time the normal buying season began, drought had hit Australia, floods had inundated northern Europe, and increased biofuel mandates had lured U.S. farmers away from devoting their land to wheat for people in favor of corn for cars.

There were scores of other economic, ecological, and political reasons for higher grain prices: a weak dollar, an increase in grain hoarding, nationalistic export bans, water scarcity, desertification, stagnant crop yields, wars, natural disasters, land grabs, and increasing demands for chicken, pizza, and beef.

So when nations across the globe called for their annual hit of hard red spring, they discovered that the so-called visible supply was far lower than usual. At which point, declared FuturesMag.com: "The bull market in grain hit hyper drive."

The markets veered into insanity and food rioters hit the streets. Money chased money, a billion people went hungry, and the emperors met in Rome to argue protocol and syntax.

Silver finished his bacon and eggs, and I followed him upstairs—beyond two sets of metal detectors, dozens of security staff, and a gaudy stained-glass image of Hermes, god of commerce, luck, and thievery. Through the colored glass that outlined the deity, I caught my first glimpse of the immense trading floor of the CME. The electronic board had already begun to glitter with green, yellow, and red numbers.

If anyone would like a moral to the story, here it is: imaginary wheat bought anywhere affects real wheat bought everywhere. Virtual food everywhere transforms real food anywhere. Even as new media prophets shout praises for the meta and the hyper and the cloud and the never-ending next, our markets convey the old truth. Nothing on Earth is more valuable than food.

Business, law, and politics have all been remade since the birth of grain futures, but bread has stayed the same.

The nature of currency itself has changed, but bread has stayed the same. No matter how many steps removed from reality the meta may take us, we still need to eat.

Nineteenth-century grain merchants perceived the enduring value of wheat and turned it into a forward contract, which evolved into a future, which evolved into an index, which evolved into a host of electronically traded derivatives and funds. Add drought, flood, and freeze. The result: bubbles.

At a grain-crisis conference in Washington, D.C., I met Larry Mitchell, a heavyset former deputy administrator of the U.S. Department of Agriculture who was then serving as vice president of government relations for the American Corn Growers. When the Iraq War began in 2003, Mitchell told me, the United States was holding eight hours' worth of soybeans and five hours' worth of corn. *Hours*—not weeks or even days.

No one at the Department of Homeland Security or the Pentagon doubted that food was a matter of national security, but as the United States deployed troops and weapons across the world, we continued to trust the global market. "Our current reserve is in the hands of multinational grain corporations," said Mitchell. "We are one disaster away from being in their hands."

The surest way to safeguard against a bad harvest or three is not a corner on virtual food, nor an intellectual license, nor an embargo or a tariff or a new tractor, but with a monstrous batch of the real thing, known as a grain reserve. In times of surging food prices, a national grain reserve can cool down overheated exchanges by bringing actual corn or actual wheat to the spot grain markets and consequently tame contango on the futures markets.

Unfortunately, the 1980s and 1990s were dominated by the dogma of unregulated global markets, and in 1993 the international General Agreement on Tariffs and Trade put an end to grain reserves as a government responsibility. The 1996 farm bill abolished the grain reserve of the United States.

Two years after my conversation with Mark Bagan, CEO of the Minneapolis Grain Exchange, the bubble business began again. Commodity futures shot up in Chicago, Kansas City, and Minneapolis, and the U.N. Food and Agriculture Organization's food price index passed the record it had set in 2008. For the second time in three years, food was more expensive than it had ever been in all of human history.

The 2011 bubble hit every sector of the commodity markets. One spring morning, cocoa futures dropped 12 percent in less than a minute. Corn hit an all-time high, and sugar futures began to swing more in one day than they used to in a month. The CME raised its margin requirements on silver five times in two days, and Howard Schultz, the CEO of Starbucks, railed against speculators in commodity coffee. PepsiCo forecast that its own medium-term commodity cost increases would exceed a billion dollars.

The world's largest food producers hired math PhDs and economic modelers to theorize and implement ever more complex hedging strategies to keep up with the second-by-second spikes and flash crashes of grain and livestock futures as high-frequency traders and momentum-driven hedge funds made it their business to speculate on food.

"The market is broken," the chief executive of one of the biggest cotton producers in the United States lamented to

the *New York Times* in the spring of that year. "It no longer
serves its purpose." Both the Kansas City Board of Trade and
the Minneapolis Grain Exchange recorded their highest electronic trading volumes in history.

The last time I visited MGEX, I asked a handful of wheat
brokers what would happen if the U.S. government banned
banks from the practice of index trading food commodities. Their reaction: laughter. All it would take would be
one phone call to a bona fide hedger like Cargill or Archer
Daniels Midland, one secret swap of assets, and a bank's
stake in the futures market would become indistinguishable
from that of an international wheat buyer.

I asked what would happen if the government outlawed *all*
indexed derivative products. Once again, the response was
laughter. The problem could be solved with another phone
call, this time to a trading office in London or Hong Kong.
For the new food derivative markets have reached suprana-
tional proportions, beyond the reach of sovereign law.

The more that financial derivatives prosper, proliferate,
and pile up on one another and the more that virtualities
masquerade as realities, the more difficult it will become
to penetrate the gilded surfaces and see what derives value
from what. Tomorrow will bring ever decreasing differences
between imagination and reality, and the subtle conflations
will be intriguing to parse. But academic ambiguities provide
a particularly dissatisfying conclusion to the tale of a billion
hungry people on Earth, particularly when there are steps we
can take to avert another global food crisis. A national grain
reserve is first. An international grain reserve is second. Then
come the regulations and reforms.

As of today, bankers and traders sit at the top of the international food chain—the carnivores of the system, devouring

everyone and everything below. Near the bottom toil the farmers. For them, the rising price of grain should have been a windfall, but speculation has also created spikes in everything the farmers must buy to grow their grain—from intellectually licensed seeds to transnational fertilizer to diesel fuel. At the very bottom of the food chain lie the consumers. Average Americans, who spend 8 to 12 percent of their weekly paychecks on food, may not immediately feel the crunch of rising costs. But for the roughly two billion people across the world who spend more than 50 percent of their income on food, the effects are staggering.

Fortunately, there is a straightforward solution to the food derivative problem: revoke the position-limit exemptions that are handed out to a few select banks by the U.S. Commodity Futures Trading Commission and enforce position limits for all the other banks, no matter where their home base. The index funds and all their relatives would disappear overnight if a bank could hold no more than five thousand futures contracts, as was the case until the year 2000.

As the global price of food peaked, I became curious about the state of the commodity markets in the World Food Program's Purchase for Progress countries. The last time I had seen Uganda's president, Yoweri Museveni, he was in New York, seated on the dais of U.N. conference room 4. That morning I had sat through a paean of gratitude as Museveni elaborated his debt to Bill Gates and the WFP—particularly regarding all that food they were buying from Uganda's largest plantations. "High food prices are very good for us," Museveni said. But he was wrong.

Two months after the Tunisian fruit and vegetable seller Muhammad Bouazizi immolated himself on the streets of Sidi Bouzid, Uganda held its presidential election. As usual, Museveni's former physician, Warren Kizza Besigye Kifefe, emerged from exile to run against his former patient. Also as usual, Besigye lost to Museveni by a wide margin—his third straight defeat. There were widespread accusations that votes had been bought for a bit of salt and ten thousand Ugandan shillings, worth about four dollars. It was central African electoral politics as usual—except for the food bubble.

"We are tired of this government because of the price of commodities," a Ugandan student complained to the *Guardian* after the April election. "There is no presidency in Uganda. He is a dictator. We need change."

In an attempt to harness widespread indignation over rising food and fuel prices, Besigye called for a "walk to work" street protest, and soon the road to Entebbe's airport was blocked. At that point Museveni's police force smashed the roadblock, sprayed tear gas into Besigye's face, and dragged the blinded fifty-five-year-old opposition leader off to prison. Then Museveni's son, Lieutenant Colonel Muhoozi Kainerugaba, rallied the Ugandan army to quell the protests blooming in Kampala. Kainerugaba's soldiers fired live bullets and canisters of tear gas and beat the demonstrators with sticks. The protesters blocked more roads, burned more tires, and threw rocks at the armored cars.

Yaneer Bar-Yam sat in his office at the New England Complex Systems Institute, a Cambridge, Massachusetts, think tank that analyzes problems previously considered beyond the reach of scientific inquiry. Bar-Yam was trained as a physicist, so he believes that on a certain level all complex systems—be they the weather, an insect colony, or a market—possess similar structures and functions.

Until recently, world food crises had been relatively rare events, occurring an average of three times a century. Now there had been two price spikes in three years, and it was clear to Bar-Yam that the equilibrium of a complex system had been disturbed. A new force had entered the markets, and Bar-Yam realized he had to try to quantify speculation.

"Welcome back, Fred," said an e-mail from BarclayHedge .com. The online hedge fund research specialists were introducing yet another agricultural traders index. Turns out that second- and third-generation food derivative products have improved on Goldman's original long-only model, and a new cottage industry of exchange-traded funds (ETFs) is upon us.

The *Dynamic Wealth Report* sent along this note:

> By now you're probably sick of hearing about it.
>
> Commodity prices are soaring across the board and if you're not making money . . . then you're being left behind!
>
> But the good news is . . . the bull market is just getting started!

A few days later another ETF e-mail blast came my way, announcing the debut of an index product that would "offer exposure to the global food and beverage industry." The next day came a teaser for an ETF index linked to global fish. Then came an offer from the PowerShares Global Water Portfolio ETF. After the heads-up on water came an offer to buy shares of an ETF based on volatility itself—perhaps the biggest bull of them all.

Many of the people I came across in my journey to understand the price of bread continue to believe that food markets illustrate the economic laws of supply and demand, rational expectations, and price equilibrium. But the crisscrossed lines that undergraduate economics professors project onto the big screens at the beginning of every semester do not describe what has happened.

Traders in food commodities like to call their market free, but it is not. We must all participate, to the tune of 2,700 calories per day. To opt out of this market means death. And that is what I learned when I went looking for a pizza and ended up on Wall Street. That is what I discovered when I learned how wheat got its price.

The benefit of wheat is not cash. The benefit of wheat is bread, and the benefit of bread is life.

Epilogue

Return to Reality

At Davos, Professor Yaneer Bar-Yam of the New England Complex Systems Institute presented sums and graphs that demonstrated what the bankers and traders had led me to understand through hints and rumors. After he finished, it was time for questions, and the CEO of one of the world's largest grain conglomerates raised his hand. I wish I could tell you his name, but such disclosure would violate the spirit of Davos.

The CEO stood up and contradicted Bar-Yam. There was no speculation in commodities, he said. There was only the push and pull of supply and demand. The market was perfect, the market was all we need. Since this was Switzerland—where everything starts and finishes on time—the session on food price came to an end before Bar-Yam could refute the refutation.

The lack of resolution of the disagreement at the World Economic Forum was typical, for there is too much at stake for the debate to disappear: too much food transformed into money, too much money masquerading as food, and too much dogma about buying and selling one or the other or both. Economic philosophy, history, and theory have attached themselves to breakfast, lunch, and dinner. You can no longer have one without the other.

I thought I had a simple question: Why can't inexpensive, healthy, and delicious food be available to everyone? As I searched for the answer, I came across countless illustrations of global food injustice. But as long as bread means nothing but money, there will be no solution. The war of words will continue, as will our oldest problem.

One day, perhaps, we will fall out of love with the virtual, and it will be clear to everyone that food is neither an index nor a code, not a derivative and not an investment. On that day we will return to reality. Food will start on the long road back to being food, and hunger will become what it has never been: something you only read about in books.

Acknowledgments

Like many projects, this book had more than one beginning. It began over drinks with Luke Mitchell, when we decided that after all the articles for *Harper's* about eating it was time to write about not having anything to eat. It began at the Los Angeles Book Fair, when I sat on the same panel as Raj Patel and heard him present findings from his book *Stuffed and Starved: The Hidden Battle for the World Food System* (2008). It began when James Oseland at *Saveur* magazine accepted an article about the genetics of fruit shape. It began when Eric Nelson at John Wiley & Sons sent me a note. It began with a chain of e-mails to and from Bonnie Nadell, a chain that keeps going.

Many others have provided support along the way: Rocco Castoro at *Vice* magazine, who was not afraid of red wine laced with jellyfish genes; Matt Marion at *Men's Health*, who took a chance on global pizza; Laura Wright, from OnEarth; and Benjamin Pauker at *Foreign Policy*. Thanks are also due to Claire Provost of the *Guardian* (U.K.); Krista DeBoer of the Harvard Food Law Society; Roger Hodge, for believing I could coax a story from a stack of statistics; Sarah Kavage, for getting the word out and making it real; and President Leonel Fernandez of the Dominican Republic, for including me in the global conversation.

Many elements of the story attracted media early on, and this focus helped mold a topic into a book. Thanks to Dylan Ratigan at MSNBC, Kevin Tibbles at *NBC Nightly News*, Pimm Fox at Bloomberg Business News, Juan Gonzales and Amy Goodman at *Democracy Now!*, Mona Zughbi at RT Networks, Eric Spinato and Charles Gasparino at Fox Business News, and Diane Hatz of TEDx Manhattan.

This book would not have been possible without the support of Steve Shepard and Judy Watson of the City University of New York's Graduate School of Journalism and Ashley Dawson and Maryann Feola of the City University of New York's College of Staten Island. Thanks to Magdalena Kropiwnicka, for making clear the obscurities of the Food and Agriculture Organization; Indrani Sen and Amartya Sen, for opening their minds to me, not to mention their home; Philip McMichael and Harriet Friedmann, for their tireless work on food regime theory; David Rieff, for endless conversation and too many espressos; Marion Nestle, for inspiration and encouragement; and Krishnendu Ray and Janet Poppendieck, for wisdom and insight.

I am grateful for the participation of many scientists and farmers, including David Tricoli, Pamela Ronald, Raoul Adamchak, Esther van der Knaap, John Johnson, Frank Muller, and Sandy Lewis. I also owe a debt of thanks to Mark Bagan and his staff at the Minneapolis Grain Exchange and to many in the food industry, including staff at Domino's, Unilever, Tyson Foods, and the Stewardship Index for Specialty Crops.

Many offered insights into history, economics, and finance, chief among them Eunice Bet-Mansour, Olivier de Scheutter, Harwood Schaffer, Darryl Ray, Paul Freedman, Roy Lennox, Andrew Kuritzkes, Steven Rothbart, Andrés Velasco, and James Barnett. Yaneer Bar-Yam of the New England Complex Systems Institute continues to make invaluable contributions.

There are those who transcend category: Eric Anderson, Hali Breindel, Elizabeth Beier, Jonathan Bulkeley, Damon Brandt, Dillon Freed, Dewitt Godfrey, Monica Burzcyk, Michael Greenberg, Joe Grutzik, Melissa Harris, George Prochnik, Rebecca Mead, and Jonathan Towers. Thank you for your wisdom, friendship, and support.

A special debt of gratitude to Andrew Leigh.

Thank you, Lorraine Kaufman, for unending generosity and love. Thank you, Millard Kaufman, for every lesson about a word that rhymes with fighting. Thank you to my children, Phoebe and Julian. And thanks beyond thanks to Lizzie, without whom none of this would be possible.

Index